Endorsen

Full Circle is a story of one woman's struggle to understand her incomparable worth in Christ. Through rejection, rebellion, and fear—until she found herself in the clutches of a cult—author Athena Dean experienced true redemption, freedom and renewal as she surrendered to Jesus. An important story for anyone who has wandered lost, longing to be found.

—Mary E. DeMuth, author of *Worth Living:*
How God's Wild Love for You Makes You Worthy

Throughout all the ups and downs Athena has experienced, the faithfulness of God shines through. Seeing the Lord's redemption in every area of her life will inspire and encourage you to yearn for the same divine touch for yourself and for everyone you hold dear.

—Dr. Dennis E. Hensley author of *Jesus in All Four Seasons*

Full Circle paints with vivid word pictures the lack we surely feel and the hunger we rarely face and almost never reveal to God, ourselves and others. Thank you, Athena for the hope you poured onto the pages that we might find the wholeness we all deserve to know, to be and to live. Bravo!

—Michele Pillar, three-time Grammy-nominated singer, speaker, and author of *Untangled: The Truth Will Set You Free*

Athena's story is incredible. She displays such courage as she opens her heart to share. I highly recommend *Full Circle*.

—Cynthia L Simmons, Heart of the Matter Radio, author of *Pursuing Gold*

Acclaimed publisher, blogger, radio show host, and pastor's wife Athena Dean Holtz's memoir, *Full Circle*, absolutely shreds the mistaken concept that good can not possibly come out of evil; that abuse—from physical to, yes, even spiritual abuse—can not possibly beautifully birth strength, wisdom, discernment, peace and pure godly-grit that brings all of life wonderfully full circle.

—Ronna Snyder, award-winning freelance magazine writer; former contributor, *Today's Christian Woman* magazine; author of *Hot Flashes from Heaven*

Brave, honest, raw. Full of wisdom forged in the fires of experience. Every reader will be enriched by Athena's open and revealing account of her journey into wholeness.

—Jennifer Kennedy Dean, executive director of The Praying Life Foundation, author of *Live a Praying Life* and numerous other books

Full Circle by Athena Dean is a must-read for any woman who, like me, grew up struggling with the need for attention. I was a Christian and well into middle-age before I realized that need continued to influence me in my decisions. This book is well written and practical in its design, which enables readers to personally apply the life applications found there. Highly recommended!

—Kathi Macias, author and speaker

Athena's story is truly like no other. You can see God's hand on her life in every page of this book. The adventures she's been on with the Lord will leave you amazed and inspired by His faithfulness through it all.

—Anna Quesada, founder of Christian Women's
Small Business Association

A whirlwind story of love, deception, darkness and triumph, Athena's memoir is touching and full of hope. Her honesty and self-disclosure makes it easy to identify with her and see ourselves in her journey of self-discovery and healing.

—Michelle Hollomon, MA, LMHC, CPC,
Licensed Mental Health Counselor, Certified Professional Coach

I was drawn into the book immediately and there I stayed until the very end—all in one day. I didn't expect it to be quite that compelling, since I know Athena well, and already knew her story. But hearing it all again in more detail, I experienced incredulity and horror, then amazement and thankfulness, as well as everything in between. Only God could orchestrate such a transformation. Talk about beauty for ashes! And that transformation continues as Athena walks out the hills and valleys of her new life.

—Gay Lewis, author of *Bittersweet: The Restoration Continues*, host
and prayer facilitator at The Hill

Ever wonder how a person can become victim to religious brain washing? In her new book, Athena shares her story. From the time she was a young girl, her longing to feel significant and special took her to depths of sorrow. Believing those who told her that aborting her baby was best sent her searching for answers. With a lifelong yearning to find God,

Athena unwittingly allowed herself to be brainwashed by a number of cults, which continually brought her to the brink of destruction. But God, who is rich in mercy, redeemed Athena's brokenness through grace and truth. Her story will help you: discern your own vulnerability to false teaching; discover the One who will fill the void in your soul; realize the importance of studying and knowing God's Word; guard against religions that twist the true meaning of Scripture; and find comfort and hope as you pray for others who are being deceived

—Rhonda Stoppe, author, *Real Life Romance*

In *Full Circle*, Athena Dean Holtz gives a vulnerable account of the path we can travel down when we try to fill "God-shaped holes" with anything but Him. Yet, just as the title suggests, she reveals how despite our misguided decisions and the lure of the enemy, God is always at work wooing His children back to Him, where He can faithfully be the healer, the provider, the sustainer, the protector, and the redeemer we all long for. This is a vital message for anyone who feels lost or abandoned by God, or who needs the assurance that nothing separates us from the love of God.

—Dr. Michelle Bengtson, speaker and author of *Hope Prevails: Insights from a Doctor's Personal Journey Through Depression*

Athena has written a compelling memoir of redemption. Her story includes domestic abuse, spiritual deception, and finally the kind of restoration that can only come when God steps in. *Full Circle: Coming Home to the Faithfulness of God* is a page-turner!

—Nick Harrison, author of *Magnificent Prayer* and *Power in the Promises*

Athena Dean's book, *Full Circle,* will draw you in as this neglected little girl searches for love and meaning in all the wrong places. Thankfully, our God is a restorer of lives and Athena's redemption story is powerful. You will not be able to put this book down!

—Lisa Burkhardt Worley, award-winning author

This book drew me in and captivated me for the next four hours. I love Athena Dean Holtz's book *Full Circle* because it is a raw and honest love story. Love in a marriage, love for success, and her quest to fully know the love of God. Athena's engaging and lively writing style shows how easily we can be deceived in our quest for what we think is right and good. This book will enthrall the reader as Athena weaves us through the depth of despair, and takes us to the heights of love and renewed hope. I highly recommend this book for personal reading and a gift to those looking for deeper faith and hope.

—Heidi McLaughlin, international speaker and author of *Restless for More, Fulfillment in Unexpected Places*

Athena has done and experienced more in her lifetime than one might think possible. She went from incredible success to unthinkable emotional slavery, nearly losing herself and everything she held dear to a controlling and destructive cult. But then God showed up, changed her thinking and surrounded her with life-changing, freedom-bringing grace. This true story is a thought-provoking and God-glorifying tale of one woman's journey of learning to live deeply and fully loved.

—Jennifer Slattery, author of *Restoring Love* and founder of Wholly Loved Ministries

I highly recommend Athena's story, *Full Circle*. It is a refreshingly honest story of one woman's search for God's best for her life. Athena and I became good friends in the early 1990s. Over the years, we would spend time together when we were both exhibitors and/or presenters at ICRS, NRB and writer's conferences. I watched the change in her when she became involved with the Williamses and rejoiced with her when she finally realized their church was a cult. She paid a high price when she left, but because of the desire of her heart for God's perfect will, He has given her a husband to love her, a ministry, and a restored business. Her story of coming back "full circle" is a must read.

— Joyce Hart Owner and CEO of Hartline Literary Agency

Warning: Do not pick up this book if you are planning something important! My plan was to read it over the weekend, but four hours later I awoke to the realization that I had been captured by a love story. It is the embrace of a Father who loves us as we travel through the minefields of the agendas of those who would use and abuse us. It is a story of victory and redemption. It also is an immersion into the murky waters of a toxic church, and an experience that through grace, the power of God redeems. This story is hope personified.

—Fred St. Laurent, CEO of The Book Club Network,
Bookfun.org and *Book Fun Magazine*

Athena's writing caught my attention when I read about her cult-like church experience some years ago. I'd gone through something similar in my family of origin, so I related. Shortly after I found her writings, she took a break from sharing her story to allow her family time to heal, and I realized how significant she'd already been to my own healing from religious abuse. I thought, *Finally, someone understands.* I felt the same sense of hope and restoration upon finishing *Full Circle.* In her book, Athena is factual about the brainwashing she experienced, transparent about her own mistakes, and grateful for God's protection as she tried to find her way back to her faith. Her story is a beautiful one of God's grace and redemption.

—S. Kim Henson, writer and blogger

The unfolding of Athena's story of redemption is one that will touch lives, bringing hope to those who are broken and needing restoration, as they too choose true repentance and obedience.

—Marlene Salcher, speaker, mentor, author of
God Speaks to Me? Tuning in to the Living God

What a testimony to God's redemptive power and restorative grace! Athena's life proves that, no matter the nature and depth of our inner wounds and pain, God is willing and able to lovingly restore. Indeed, He brings beauty from ashes.

—Grace Fox, international speaker and author of *Moving from
Fear to Freedom: A Woman's Guide to Peace in Every Situation*

In *Full Circle*, you'll read a story of a heroine who encounters many trials, hardships, broken hearts and moments of joy that take her on a journey she never could have imagined. And it's all true! I met Athena after she had received Christ but was in the grips of a cult (which, by the way, none of us knew at the time, including Athena). After I would speak with her, I would walk away thinking, there is something holding her back, she isn't ever fully herself. I surmised she was an introvert (oh, how wrong I was). It wasn't long before I watched Athena break free. It was like watching a butterfly struggle and battle to get out of a cocoon. From the cocoon of abuse, cults and all emerged this beautiful woman of God. A woman God had been pursuing all her life. A woman the enemy didn't want found. But God is faithful. Deuteronomy 4:29 (NASB) promises: "But from there you will seek the Lord your God, and you will find Him if you search for Him with all your heart and all your soul." And Psalm 22:26 (NASB): "The afflicted shall eat and be satisfied; those who seek Him will praise the Lord." Athena began to seek for the true God and she found Him because, as she does everything, she was in with her whole heart and whole soul. Once afflicted, she now eats at the Father's table and is satisfied and praise resounds. Loving pursuit, redemption, forever after . . . ah, the stuff that princess tales are made of. Enjoy!

—Kim Bangs, senior acquisitions editor,
Bethany House and Chosen Books

Toxic spiritual abuse nearly destroyed Athena, and yet God's redemption is woven through her story. His faithfulness rescued her, and the obedience to listen to the whisper of God's truth led her out of a destructive cult. Satan is masterful at weaving lies with a little bit of truth for the purpose of distorting God's character. Athena reminds us how easy it is to stray if we don't know His truth for ourselves and the consequences of unhealthy dependence on others. Her story is a brilliant reminder of God's unfathomable grace to all of us. *Full Circle* will capture your heart and reminds you to stay close to Jesus, ever listening for his voice.

—Cynthia Cavanaugh, author, speaker, and life coach

You can't help but have God speak directly to your heart while reading Athena's words in *Full Circle: Coming Home to the Faithfulness of God.* Prepare to be humbled by Athena's vulnerability. Prepare to have God shine a spotlight on the cracks in your faith. Prepare to be changed.

—Bethany Jett, award-winning author of *The Cinderella Rule: A Young Woman's Guide to Happily Ever After*

FULL CIRCLE

Coming Home to the Faithfulness of God

FULL CIRCLE

Coming Home to the Faithfulness of God

Athena Dean Holtz

with Inger Logelin

REDEMPTION
PRESS

Published by Redemption Press, PO Box 427, Enumclaw, WA 98022

Toll Free (844) 2REDEEM (273-3336)

Redemption Press is honored to present this title in partnership with the author. The views expressed or implied in this work are those of the author. Redemption Press provides our imprint seal representing design excellence, creative content, and high quality production.

ISBN 13: 978-1-68314-237-9 (Print)
978-1-68314-238-6 (ePub)
978-1-68314-239-3 (Mobi)

Library of Congress Catalog Card Number: 2017931949

Dedication

To my faithful King, who redeemed my life from the pit.
To my knight in shining armor who loves me well.
To my children, who've journeyed with me through my healing.
To the Holtz clan, who embraced me wholeheartedly.
To my church family at The Summit EFC for welcoming me
as the new pastor's wife.
And to all those who have suffered spiritual abuse and toxic leadership
. . . may my story of redemption give you hope.

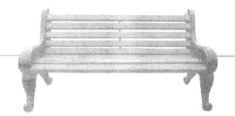

Contents

Home is something I ran from—the ties—the disapproval—the hypocrisy. I wanted to be on stage . . . I wanted the acclamation and attention I got from performing—from being out front—from being *seen*. I pulled away from my parents—especially my mom—husband—children—into the arms of what I thought would bring me happiness.

Along the way, I allowed myself to be deceived—by abuse, Scientology, mysticism, and eventually twelve years in a restrictive, legalistic cult posing as a church that took everything from me.

This is my story of how God brought me full circle. How He brought me *home* . . . to a place I had always longed for, but never knew how to find.

Athena Dean Holtz

January 2017

I woke up groggy from the anesthesia, clutching my empty abdomen.

My baby . . . my baby was gone.

My soft center, the place where my heart should be, felt like a rock.

I will not cry. I will not cry.

The man who said he loved me was gone. He started
walking away . . . easing out . . . when I told him about the baby.

I guess he isn't going to leave his wife for me after all.

Used. I feel used, like a crumpled old tissue.

"Your life will be ruined, Athena. The last thing you need is a baby."

No. The last thing I need is to trust anyone.

I'll never let anyone use me again.

ONE

See Me!

All bad behavior is really a request for love, attention, or validation.
—Kimberly Giles, *Choosing Clarity: The Path to Fearlessness*

In the slightly out-of-focus, old black-and-white photo, I'm a blond two-year old on my mom's lap . . . reaching out . . . unhappy . . . wanting to be elsewhere. Her attention is fully focused on my quiet and calm brother at her side, while I look desperate to be elsewhere.

Where did it all start—that pulling away from my mom, that need for the next thing?

My father wasn't in the photo. *Was I reaching out for him?*

I knew my dad, Arthur L. Sikking Jr., loved me, maybe because I was the only girl. Or was it because he saw his own traits in me? Like him, I was outgoing and craved attention.

Dad found affirmation in his success in sales. I didn't know it when I was a child, but Dad was one of the best salesmen ever. A self-made man, he started out selling door-to-door and worked his way up to becoming vice president of sales for Encyclopedia Britannica, making record-breaking achievements and seven figures a year.

What mattered to me was being with him, not always a frequent occurrence. When I did see him, I wanted him to *see me*—Athena.

See *me!* See *me*, Dad! I'd dance and twirl and laugh and try to catch his eye. I wanted to be the center of attention, his special girl. He'd bring out his movie camera with the blinding bank of lights across the top, and I'd come to life. He'd sing me silly songs from old commercials and tell me stories about himself.

When he was home, which wasn't often, he would pay attention to me and spoil me. He said I made him laugh. "There's my girl," he'd say. I *was* his girl. He'd look in my eyes and say, "If there were a thousand little girls in a big field, and I flew over in my helicopter, I would look and look until I found *you*. And I would pick *you* out of all the other 999. You know why? Because you're special. Because you are you."

Athena Daphne Sikking was born on March 28, 1953. Yes, that's me! It seems I was difficult for my mom from the start. We were living in Honolulu as Dad was selling encyclopedias there for Colliers. Allergic to milk, I was fed poi. Mom told me I almost choked on the cereal made from taro root more than once. I've wondered if my bond would have been different with my mom if she had breastfed me. Maybe it wasn't done in our social circles.

I was the little girl who spilled India ink on a valuable oriental carpet while visiting my grandma's house and killed the tropical fish by turning up the heat on the tank. Naturally curious and full of energy, I was a handful.

Because of Dad's drive to succeed in his career, and his workaholism, we enjoyed the fruits of his labor, while seeing less and less of him. With my father's business success came the demands of frequent travel.

The Sikkings, Dad's family, were mostly Dutch. In the Great Depression of the 1930s, the family struggled financially, losing their home in 1934, but later became well off as my grandfather worked in engineering, and grandmother rose in status as a minister in the Unity church.

Mom, Angela Seraph Sikking, was Greek—hence the origin of my name. She was a reserved and unemotional, dark-haired beauty, an elegant entertainer, and a perfectionist. Mom made sure our façade was presentable—her makeup, clothes, hair, of course, and the house, the decor, the meals. Impressing people was important to both Mom and Dad who cared deeply about appearances. But the ideal marriage and family were not within her ability to arrange.

My parents' marriage was a sham. When Dad would come home, he'd be the life of the party; but the party was over for my mom. Dad was leading a double life with ongoing relationships with other women. When I was about eleven or twelve, he fell in love with a flight attendant named Kathy, and the relationship lasted until he passed away at age eighty-one.

When Mom found out about Dad's relationship, she just made him move into a different bedroom. She didn't divorce him. They'd go out together socially—to see and be seen and keep up the sham of their showcase home and family.

Dad spent as much time as he could with his new love and at home became an absentee father. When I did see him, I tried hard to win his approval. He was my sun, my solar system, and I needed the warmth of his full attention and approval.

Atlanta was home from age one to eight; my only memories from there come from the home movies Dad took when he showed up. As I got older, it felt as if the attention Dad was paying me was just for show. *He says he loves me, but he's going to leave again.* I felt starved for his words of affirmation—anything that would make me feel special and unique. He gave me that affirmation at times, but the words didn't feel real when he left us again.

I wasn't the kind of little girl who played with baby dolls or played house. Those things didn't interest me. I didn't dream and play make-believe about growing up and having a cozy home and children with me as the mommy. I just wanted to stand out from the crowd and win approval. At school, I was competitive, always trying to outdo my peers, and win in all the games we played—and I usually did. Being the best was important to me. While I got along well with my peers, I'm sure that got old.

My brother Jim is three years my elder, while my younger brother, Arthur Leland Sikking III, was born when I was eight. The addition of my younger brother just cemented my position as the only girl. Because of the age difference, he and I never had much of a connection.

In Chicago, our second home was in one of the most affluent suburbs in a million-dollar house with an indoor swimming pool. Dad had a helicopter he'd land on the hockey field of my private school in Wisconsin to pick me up for weekend horse shows.

My passion in childhood was horses, so my parents started me on lessons at age eleven. I'd get to the horse barn early in the morning and ride after school every day. The equestrian world gave me an opportunity to shine, to compete and excel. I always wanted to be the best in my class. I rode hunters, and at one time had seven horses; two were my dad's, but I rode them when he was away. When I began competing in horse shows, showing four of them every weekend, I was hooked! My parents were fully behind me and never seemed to regret the expenses and time it required. Being highly competitive himself, Dad wanted to give me the opportunity to succeed at competitive riding.

My drive to please my father by winning the blue ribbon became an obsession. Once when my dad was in town for a rare appearance at my horse show, I finished a round with a perfect score. I looked out into the stands, caught his eye, and saw him give me a big smile and a "thumbs up." A warmth filled me inside and a sense of satisfaction. I had pleased my father!

By the time I was eighteen, my winning streak in horse shows had taken me across the Midwest, and I had gone national at the all-star horse show at Madison Square Garden. That was my last show, and I was showing my third horse, "Isle of Erin," a grand champion. Dad bought her for $15,000, and shortly after showing her at the Gardens, sold her for $30,000. She was then shown by George Morris, famous in the horse world, and sold for $150,000 in the 1970s.

At holidays, Dad was the life of the party, but it felt like it was all show. Most of the time, Dad wasn't there, and I felt empty without his approval. When we were together, he'd pump me up by telling me, "You can do anything you want to do if you just want it bad enough." I had everything material I wanted, but I didn't have him or his full attention most of the time. *Would Dad still love me if I didn't win?* I wondered.

My relationship with my mom wasn't good. She found me excitable, strong-willed, always causing a ruckus, like my dad. She wanted me to be like my big brother, Jim, who was docile, calm, and compliant . . . like her.

When I was five years old and living in Georgia, something happened that would change my young life. Our black maid, Odessa, began sexually molesting me. She'd say, "Little girl, this is our secret."

I didn't tell. I only have the conscious memory of one incident but know the abuse was ongoing until we moved to New York when I was eight. Those three years are mercifully like a blank page in my life; I can't remember much from those years. But the seeds of sensuality had been sown into my young life.

Mom never knew what happened, and Dad wasn't there much. I didn't turn toward my mom for comfort, but away. We were so different from each other. Mom was critical and demanding. I was messy, leaving each room looking like a tornado had swept through. I was loud; she was quiet. Did my outgoing personality traits remind her of my father, whose womanizing had left her to raise us practically alone in a loveless marriage?

She did come to every horse show and even every practice session. She'd keep a sharp eye on me to make sure I did everything exactly right. "Athena, keep your toes in and your heels down." Or, "Sit up straight! You look like a slouch!"

I'm sure she thought she was doing this for my good, but it communicated rejection to my young heart. *You're not doing it right. You're not good enough. You have to try harder!*

Jim, reserved and cooperative, didn't give her trouble. He was an A student who enjoyed the same things she did—classical music, opera, and intellectual pursuits.

I was the strong-willed child who always wanted my own way. Maybe I sensed her ambivalence about me so I'd push her to the limits of her patience. I'd choose clothes she didn't approve of and exasperate her at the dinner table by not following the correct rules of etiquette. I don't think I ever set out to please her, only my dad.

Without the constant, reassuring presence of my father, I turned elsewhere. By the time I was a young teenager, my rebellious attitude had morphed me into a boy-crazy wild child who craved attention from the opposite sex. When we'd visit my aunt and uncle in Huntsville, my cousin Kerrie and I would dance around on the balcony playing Sonny and Cher music at full blast to try to get the attention of the boys in the neighborhood. Unfortunately, the only attention my cousin got was from Uncle Henry and his leather belt.

I didn't know what my dad and uncle meant when I heard them joking about me having "bedroom eyes." I just knew I loved boys. My friends and I became groupies of The Meads, a local Chicago band. If I could be sung to from the stage, I felt as if I had arrived. Knowing the "in" people—the band—the ones in the spotlight—made me feel important and significant. After all, if I knew the guy on stage who everyone wanted to know, that made me special . . . right?

Studying and school didn't rank high on my list of choice activities. I'd get in trouble for talking too much. My mind was on riding my horses and showing them on the weekends. Homework was not important to me, nor was trying to fit into the cool cliques. I didn't even go to my high school graduation; I was competing at a horse show instead.

My friends and I were beginning to experiment with LSD, mescaline, marijuana, and hash. We'd cruise bars, and I'd look for guys to flirt with, usually from the band, to make me feel special. The trauma of my molestation had sown seeds of sensuality and promiscuity that erupted in my late teens.

At nineteen and in my first half year of college, I got pregnant by the lead guitar player in a well-known Chicago-area band. I was determined to keep the baby. The baby's father had told me, again and again, "I'm going to marry you. I'm going to leave my wife and marry you." *Maybe he will keep his promise if I have the baby.*

But I knew he was already easing out of the relationship and the responsibility of a child.

Three months pregnant, I finally admitted my predicament to my parents.

My dad was dead set against me having this baby. "No way, Athena," my dad lectured. "Your life would be ruined. The last thing you need is the responsibility of a baby. I will make the necessary arrangements. I'll take care of everything."

I had no idea what this decision would do to me emotionally, but I allowed my dad to take over and clean up my mess.

I had an abortion at a hospital under general anesthesia, though this was still an illegal procedure in 1972.

The day afterwards, I lay, heartbroken, in my little brother's bed in his room, nearly delirious with a raging fever from toxemia.

My parents had moved into a small condo without a room for me. Somehow, that no-room-for-me thing was symbolic of my life then.

Deeply hurt, I felt taken advantage of and used. I didn't allow myself to feel the depths of the pain of the loss of my baby, the betrayal of the broken relationship, or the abortion. I hardened my heart. *I will protect myself.*

That's when I made the vow.

I will never let anyone use me again.

TWO

Filling the Vacuum

What else does this craving, and this helplessness, proclaim but that there was once in man a true happiness, of which all that now remains is the empty print and trace?

This he tries in vain to fill with everything around him, seeking in things that are not there, the help he cannot find in those that are, though none can help, since this infinite abyss can be filled only with an infinite and immutable object; in other words, by God himself.

—Blaise Pascal[1]

I was not one of those little girls who dreamed of getting married and settling down. No baby buggies and house with a white picket fence for me! I wanted significance.

My family dynamics and relationships set me up for a life of striving to be special . . . an unquenchable desire to be affirmed. Affirmation brought me comfort and dulled the pain from the trauma in my life. Important to me were money, success, ambition, and even notoriety.

I didn't realize my forays into all types of spirituality were my attempts to fill up the God-sized empty spot in my heart.

---

[1] Blaise Pascal, *Pensees* (New York: Penguin Books, 1966), 75.

Our family roots were New Age from my father's mother, my grandmother, Sue Sikking. My mom was not religious at all, despite her family being staunch Greek Orthodox. I sensed something happened in her childhood that turned her away from the truth of the goodness of God, but we had never talked about it.

When I was young I had encountered a sense of the presence of God at a Christmas Eve mass at my cousin's Catholic church in Huntsville, Alabama. I felt something holy—sacred—and *other* in the service. It felt as if God was drawing me, but I didn't know who He was. *Does this mean I should become a nun?* I entertained the idea for a while, but when I learned nuns couldn't have boyfriends, I gave that idea up as I had already begun noticing the opposite sex.

I had never been to vacation Bible school as a child, or Sunday school; the closest was a confirmation class at the local Episcopal church. After I shared my short-lived interest in spiritual things, Mom thought the classes would be a good thing for me to do. Not much stuck. I don't recall hearing anything about Jesus dying for me or having a relationship with Him. Once the class was over, it was on to more exciting things!

Whenever we'd visit my grandma in Santa Monica, I'd feel a draw to her new-age Unity church, but the pull never seemed to last long. Although three out of five of my father's siblings became Unity ministers, my dad was a God hater after his best friend, who was serving in the army, was decapitated by a guillotine wire while he was riding in a Jeep. He'd say, "If God would let that happen, I don't want to know him!"

So, without a Christian influence, I filled the vacuum in my heart with other options.

After my abortion, I dropped out of college, left home and never looked back. Moving out West, I lived with my Grandma Sue at her huge home overlooking the Santa Monica beach, originally built for the silent screen star Mary Pickford. Grandma was a well-known Unity minister who was featured on the *This is Your Life* TV program with Ralph Edwards on January 1, 1958. (On a clip of the program, my five-year old blond self can be seen decked out in a fancy dress with many stiff petticoats, grabbing for the microphone stand—a foretaste of my love of the media.)

Grandma drove a Mercedes and catered to the movie stars at her church, Unity by the Sea, in Santa Monica. Attracted by the teaching, I followed in her footsteps in the new-age Unity faith. When that wasn't exciting enough, I checked out eastern meditation.

The enemy used my hunger to know God to draw me into his lies. Because I didn't know the truth, I was easy prey for the counterfeit.

I dabbled in many other new-age practices over the next twelve years or so, including the Great White Brotherhood, the Ascended Masters, and channeling, and the "new wisdom" spoken through Elizabeth Clare Prophet. If it was "out of the norm" or "cutting edge," not normal or drab, it drew me. It made me feel unique. I wanted to *know and experience*! But none of these practices filled the need in my soul, the hunger for God He had placed there.

Part of the Southern California scene I loved was the people—those quirky, edgy people—and I enjoyed edging a little closer to them. My day job was in the music business where the cool people were. I was addicted to being associated with famous people—they made me feel significant by association. First, I went to work for the business manager for Chaka Khan & Rufus, who seemed like quite the con man; then for Helen Reddy's husband, Jeff Wald, a short man with a bully complex, who was her business manager. I stayed in a desert commune for six months led by a creepy guy named Paul. Paul was sort of a guru, had rotten teeth and greased-back hair, and was about sixty-five or seventy then. People flocked to him for his way-out wisdom, which I found out later was based on Scientology.

When a famous actor, Wings Hauser, and his wife, showed me the e-meter and how it ostensibly helped people deal with what was ruining their lives, I was drawn to the other-world glitter of Scientology. The need to belong and the emptiness in my heart that had never found full acceptance in my family or home looked for it in a cause. Scientology's mission was to "clear the planet." Now there was a cause bigger than I was!

For the first five years, I spent my time promoting the ideas of the organization as the answer to all our problems on planet Earth. I spent a total of seven years heavily involved in Scientology's elite Celebrity Centre, where celebs the likes of John Travolta, Chick Corea, Al Jarreau, Karen Black, and Priscilla Presley were given their services. The big names gave the cult credibility. After all, if famous actors are in Scientology, it must be all right! It was exciting—heady even—to be associated with important people. And we were all involved in working for the cause—and supposedly making a difference together. But we were all being used as pawns to work for next to nothing and make the organization and its founder rich.

I married "Carl," an ethics officer—sort of a cult cop—in the Sea Org, the full-time volunteer organization of Scientology. Carl had a "cool factor" as he exercised power and authority over the minions in the organization. After we were married, anger began to emerge that totally negated his cool factor. The beatings started soon after we were married, and within the first few weeks, I was wearing my first black eye. That progressed to him hitting me on the side of the head in the car and bursting my eardrum.

I wasn't aware of the label of "domestic violence" back in the late 1970s and early 80s. Before I met Carl, the thought of a man striking a woman and injuring her was foreign to me.

"I'm really sorry," he'd say after he cooled down. "It won't happen again, I promise."

Taken in by his words, I tried to make it work. Words of affirmation and physical touch are my "love languages" and he knew just what to say to twist the fault and make me feel guilty.

Finally ready to leave Scientology, we fled in the middle of the night, not wanting to get caught leaving. We headed home to my folks in Chicago, and then got settled just minutes from my parents' condo in our own place. At first it was nice to be out of Scientology and living normally. But my life got way more complicated when I discovered I was pregnant. I was twenty-six and definitely did not consider myself mom material.

My parents were very involved in my life when my son, Garrett, was first born. I didn't have any idea how to be a mom, so it helped to have my own mom around for a while. That got old fast as she continued to be critical and negative. Life was complicated as both my mom and my dad's mistress wanted to be in my life and bond with the grandbaby. Then both began complaining to me about the way things were with my dad. I told each of them at different times, "If you don't like it, then leave him!"

Finally, we moved back to California—and Scientology—to get away from all the family drama. To get back into good standing with Scientology, we had to "make amends." I was no longer allowed to be on staff or employed in the Celebrity Center, but we were back in the Scientology culture and the group of friends we had something in common with.

The physical and emotional abuse escalated with the birth of our second son, Aaron, and our marriage fell apart after only four years. Never in my wildest imagination would I have thought my husband would break my arm while I was nursing my six-month-old son. But it happened.

Convinced that relationships were dangerous, I hid myself in my work after the divorce. *I'll just have to take care of myself* I vowed. Building a successful fund-raising business was my way to self-medicate for the pain that engulfed my soul. In a subconscious attempt to numb myself, I worked tirelessly, most often seventy and eighty hours a week as I experimented with the heady and addicting drug of business success.

One day, my roommate, Pat Silverman, casually mentioned, "You need to meet my friend, Chuck Dean. But don't fall for him, he'll break your heart."

Chuck was one of the "big shot" salesmen on staff at the Advanced Org in Scientology. Intrigued, I took up the challenge. We married about two months later on Valentine's Day 1982. I hardly knew Chuck—didn't even know he was a Vietnam veteran with PTSD. He was handsome, and I made the leap. I did know he had a son and a daughter, Ailen and Roby. I quickly discovered Chuck's drive and motivation to work were not the same as mine. *I'll take care of him and me—his two kids and my two boys—no problem.* As the primary breadwinner, I immersed myself in my work, pursuing financial success rather than my family and relationships.

Because of my own wounding, my life as a mother was rife with failure. Instead of taking my role seriously, I allowed nannies and day care, and then my new husband, to raise my children. I loved my sons but never felt I had the knack of mothering. I didn't even feel guilty about it; I was just happy to escape to the world of work.

The practices and manipulative behavior in Scientology were becoming more than Chuck and I wanted to be a part of. We knew people who were told to cut off contact with their families if they were hostile to Scientology, and I'd experienced it when I left Scientology the first time. People who didn't tow the party line ended up doing a lot of the grunt work, such as cleaning floors with a toothbrush, and were allowed little sleep. Children ran wild and were kept in unsanitary conditions in Sea Org housing. With parents working twelve-to-fourteen-hour days, six days a week, their kids were often neglected. If someone left the organization, they'd be labeled an SP (suppressive person) and their reputations smeared by the Guardian's Office, Scientology's legal arm that threatened and bullied anyone who did not comply.

After being married for a year, Chuck talked me into moving up to Washington where he'd been raised. By then we had started working together in the financial services industry after being recruited by one of Chuck's old friends.

True to form, I began pouring myself into this new business. Chuck said, "I feel like you have another lover," and lost interest in the work. Once we were settled in the Pacific Northwest, he decided he'd just stay home and take care of the kids and let me have my love affair with work. In the Seattle area, we were still heavily involved in the Scientology culture. But the glitter was beginning to fade as we saw more and more hypocrisy in the leadership. We were never allowed to question how the organization was being run, but what had seemed like truth, was increasingly seeming deceptive. We were no longer the gung-ho loyalists to L. Ron Hubbard we had been in the past.

In a rented house where we lived, I stumbled onto a book entitled *White Witchcraft* by Aleister Crowley, the British occultist who founded his own religion, Thelema, and brought Satanism to America from the U.K. When I read a whole page written by Crowley that L. Ron Hubbard claimed as his own writing, I realized Scientology was all a farce.

We didn't buy into the rhetoric anymore and realized we had been duped. Finally, we'd had enough and wanted out. Chuck and his buddy wrote a booklet that made fun of the church and called them out at the same time. That was considered a blatant attack on the "church" of Scientology, and our children were dismissed from the Scientology school they were attending. We took a stand and spoke to a reporter accusing Scientology of throwing our kids out of their school, and it made the Los Angeles papers.

One day Chuck got a phone call in the phone room where he was selling a year's supply of trash bags to raise money for the nonexistent non-profit he was running with a friend.

"You are dead," a voice said before the call disconnected.

He was employing lots of Scientologists in the phone room for the so-called non-profit, so it was perceived as a threat when we pulled away. We were immediately cut off from all our friends. Being cut off from friends and family in the organization was usually enough of a threat to keep Scientologists who questioned the organization quiet. A spokesman for the "church" said we made a habit of attacking the church. We were out and free of the manipulation and shaming of the cult, but had lost our friends and our frame of reference.

Though I had worked and paid to make the planet "clear," my own heart was definitely not clear, and the God-shaped hole inside was still unfilled.

THREE

Meeting Jesus

You will seek me and find me when you seek me with all your heart.
—Jeremiah 29:13

I was thirty-three when I met Jesus.

Chuck and I had been married for four years. It was 1986, and I was making big money in insurance and securities, most months ranking in the top 2 percent of the company. God began to surround me with Christians in my new business venture. Looking back, I cringe when I think of how I must have sounded to them. At that point in my life, I considered Christians wimps and people who needed a crutch, so I wasn't the least bit interested in any of this Jesus nonsense.

But God had other plans. He's very good at finding effective ways to get our attention when He wants to.

"Athena, do you realize you took the Lord's name in vain thirty-four times in that one-hour presentation?"

As one of my reps lovingly pointed out my blind spots, I was shocked to hear I'd said "God" in a derogatory manner that many times during my talk. The Lord was beginning to awaken my awareness of Him and my sinful state. At that time in my life, I literally talked like a trucker, dropping "F" bombs galore and cussing up a storm. Swearing like a sailor was a big part of the Scientology culture I'd immersed myself in for the previous seven years, along with drinking lots of coffee and alcohol and smoking three packs of cigarettes a day.

We'd been living in Washington State for about three years by then, having removed ourselves from any proximity to the Southern California scene. I was still spending all my time working the financial services business. Chuck had opened the fund-raising business in a house in Queen Anne, close to the Space Needle. We worked in two different worlds, but at least, for once it seemed he was willing to hold down a job, and I wasn't the only one making money in the family.

As I mindlessly drove from home to the office to give our weekly opportunity presentation, KIRO radio filled the car with noise to help me distract myself from thinking about anything too deep. Then I heard the words, "Chuck and Athena Dean." I turned the radio up when I heard our names, shocked to hear a smooth radio voice say, "Chuck and Athena Dean . . . indicted for the largest charity fraud case in Washington history." I could not believe my ears. *Neighborhood Outreach was Chuck's business, not mine! How could they possibly be dragging me into this? It can't be!*

Chuck had learned a fund-raising model I'd passed on to him from my father and some of his Encyclopedia Britannica friends. After getting set up, he hooked up with another Vietnam vet friend and together they got involved in the Freemen movement—a bunch of folks who thought they shouldn't have to pay taxes and didn't need a license to drive on the roads or a social security number to work in this free country. He went as far as taking the license plates off his car and attaching some homemade ones that said, "JUST SKIP IT."

Obviously, the government didn't agree with him and didn't want to "skip it."

As Chuck got more and more involved with this mentality, he decided he didn't want to deposit the funds from his fund-raising business in a normal bank but instead used what was called a "warehouse bank" that backed all deposits with gold and silver, as opposed to federal reserve notes. He also decided he didn't have to fill out the proper forms to participate in fund-raising activities in our state. As a result, the government considered all the money he raised from the sales his company was making as fraudulent—to the tune of $250,000!

As the Washington State attorney general's office began to investigate Chuck's business, they deemed the warehouse bank "money laundering." His non-profit was deemed a "fraudulent fundraising activity."

As Chuck's involvement in the radical Freemen movement caused scrutiny of our finances, my job was on the line. I worked with the A.L. Williams company, selling term insurance and mutual funds. Now, because the word "fraud" was mentioned in the media regarding the investigation, I was in big trouble. You can't sell mutual funds and be licensed with the SEC and have anything to do with fraudulent activities!

I was furious. *I am just done with our relationship if it's going to threaten my career.* All I wanted at that point was a divorce. My business and financial success meant more to me by then than my husband and family, and he was threatening that success. *I'm making over $100,000 a year; I'll get along without him just fine.*

"What do you think you are doing, Chuck?" I screamed at him at home. We were on the opposite sides of this issue, and I didn't see a middle ground. "This relationship is over!"

During that year, I had already threatened several times to kick Chuck out. But now with the IRS and state attorney general's office paying him a call, I was furious.

I walked into our house one afternoon after a weekend away at a business retreat, with my mind made up that our marriage was over. But something about Chuck seemed different. He had been crying for days and pretty much on the verge of a breakdown. But now he was calm instead of upset and anxious. *What's going on with him?* There was a peace about him that hadn't been there before.

When my business associate called a few hours later, he told me, "Chuck has accepted Christ as his Lord and Savior."

"What? Chuck? A Christian? No way!"

Becoming a Christian was the last thing I expected. We had agreed Christians were losers and wimps. *Why would he do something so lame? Who needs a crutch like Jesus?*

We had been in and out of Scientology, the Church Universal Triumphant, meditation, astrology, and channeling! *And now he wants to be a Jesus freak? I'm still divorcing him.*

As I observed Chuck, I couldn't deny there had been a major change in him. Whatever it was, I found myself drawn to it. Three days later, I felt my heart softening. I heard myself saying to him, "Well, maybe we can give our marriage one more chance. I guess you don't have to go."

To be on the same page, I figured I'd eventually have to become one of *those* Christians too. *What will people think of me?* I worried, as everyone knew what I thought of Christians. I didn't want to appear weak. For someone who had such disdain for "those people," it was amazing I was considering becoming one of them. *After all, I thought, now that my husband is a Christian, I guess I will have to be one too. I* remembered the times when people involved in the company leadership were recognized by the company and they'd boldly credit Jesus for their success. *Oh, puh . . . leeeeze!* I would roll my eyes to express my disgust, thinking, *Alright, already . . . next!*

I was one of the few women senior vice presidents in the company. *I'm not a loser and I don't want to be one!*

But I began to read *Mere Christianity* by C. S. Lewis and then listened to a cassette tape recording of the book, and God softened my heart. I knew if we were going to stay married, I needed to be one of *them* too—whatever that meant!

Five weeks after Chuck got saved, I called Mike, my national sales director in the financial services business. He was the one who'd sent me *Mere Christianity,* and I knew I needed to meet with him. When we met that same day, I asked him, "Can you pray with me? I know I need to say this prayer to get saved. I don't know exactly how to do it."

With Mike's help, I prayed and gave my life over to Jesus and asked Him to take control. After we prayed, in an instant I was a new person—I felt washed clean for the first time in my life. I was overwhelmed with a relief that came from knowing God had forgiven me for all the rebellion and sin in my life.

What happened next was nothing short of a miracle. That foul mouth of mine was gone. The continual cursing and "F" bombs that were second nature to me disappeared, never to return. God had performed a miracle in my life by softening my hard heart, cleaning up my mouth, and drawing me to Himself. I believe even then He had a plan for me to speak for Him, so His first order of business with me was to wash my mouth out with some Holy Spirit soap.

Another thing that could be considered a miracle was the dismissal of the charity fraud indictment against us. At the hearing, some months after the indictment, Chuck admitted his errors and explained he had shut down his non-profit, was no longer using the warehouse bank, and had cut off his association with the Freemen. After it was determined his actions were not malicious, the indictment was dismissed, and a fine was levied. As a couple of new believers just learning how to pray, we were thanking God!

Yes, I was born again, a new person, now a member of God's family. But with no foundation or understanding of the Bible, my experience stayed on the surface. Somehow I felt if I surrendered everything to Jesus, He would ask me to give up everything I loved and wanted—and that was still wealth and recognition.

I'm not ready for that. I may not have articulated it, but in my heart of hearts, I wanted *my* kingdom to come and *my* will to be done—on earth. Heaven could wait. I had worked too hard to leave the fruit of my competitive striving for success and recognition.

The people I was involved with in my business had become my family. They made me feel good, and I wasn't about to give that up for anyone, not even for the Lord. They gave me the strokes that made me feel good and never asked me hard questions about how my relationships with my husband and children were going. They didn't question my motives for working seventy hours a week.

All my social life revolved around the business. If a person didn't help build my business, I didn't waste my time working on a relationship with that person.

Time spent with the children was minimal, as they didn't help me make money. I shoved down the feeling that I was failing them by staying away from them.

"Mom, when will you be home? You're never home." The kids looked sad when I'd leave them.

Though Chuck and I now had Christ in common, we were still married singles.

One day he came home all fired up to go on the mission field, I said, "Great. I hope *you* have a good time. I'm not going."

And that was the end of that!

FOUR

Doing Myself Good

Commit to the Lord whatever you do, and he will establish your plans.
—Proverbs 16:3

Like my dad, I was a born saleswoman, and could pretty much sell the proverbial ice to Eskimos. When I am sold on something, it's easy for me to share it with everyone, with energy, charisma, excitement, and a great big smile! It was easy for me to persuade others to follow me in things I could be passionate about. Nothing was ever dull, and I rarely did any job that was boring.

It wasn't only the money, accolades, and prestige, all my business ventures had an element of righting perceived wrongs. My sense of justice made me get involved when I saw people being taken advantage of, and I wanted to make things right.

Looking back, my first business was started because I felt the company I worked for took advantage of the non-profits they raised money for, so I started a company that set up a percentage to the non-profit rather than a flat fee. My second business was fueled by a desire to right a wrong by helping people who were being taken advantage of by insurance companies.

I had been saved for eighteen months when I began to feel uneasy about my work being an idol. The over $100,000 a year I was making was no longer bringing me satisfaction. We were even considering moving back to California because the top earners I worked with there were now making twice the income I was. While Christ was my Savior, money, not Jesus, was my Lord.

After I heard a teaching by Phil Israelson, I began to pray daily: "Your will, not mine, Lord. Have Your way. Use me, Lord. Change my heart to desire Your will. Show me my heart as *You* see it, not as I do." And God began to answer that prayer.

Chuck enrolled in Cascade Bible College in Bellevue, Washington. While there he heard about Point Man Ministries, a Christian outreach for Vietnam veterans, originally founded by a Vietnam vet who went into prisons and ministered to vets. Chuck's heart was to reach out to other vets after being healed of his own post-traumatic stress symptoms when he became a believer.

The widow of Point Man's founder heard about Chuck's zeal to evangelize Vietnam veterans so she asked him to take over the reins as the executive director and offered to give him the 501(c)(3) her late husband had established.

One night as I listened to Chuck give his testimony in a church, I wept as he shared. I had been so busy doing "my thing" that I didn't even know what was going on in his life. He had literally led hundreds of men to the Lord since he got saved.

I felt the Lord speaking quietly to my heart.

Walk away from the business and help Chuck in the ministry.

The voice seemed so clearly to be from God, but fear immediately set in. *That can't be God. He wouldn't want us to give up what we're living on.*

At the end of the meeting, a woman approached me who didn't have a clue about our situation and told me, "Don't be surprised if your plans change." I was stunned. God *was* speaking to me.

I knew then the Lord was asking me to leave the financial services business behind and help my husband in the ministry. I would go into full time-ministry with him, helping veterans and their family members find answers to their PTSD symptoms by including Jesus in the equation, rather than the learn-to-cope-with-it drug solution they got from the Veteran's Administration.

The fact that the ministry income was about $500 a month slowed me down a bit. How were we—a family of six with three growing boys still at home (our daughter was transitioning out of the house)—going to make it on that? But I had prayed, "Your will, not mine" and God was changing my heart.

After I transferred over my financial services business to my up-line director, my mind began churning with ideas for raising money for Point Man—grant applications and a mass mailing to raise support. But when we asked the Lord for strategies, we only heard, *Pray.*

Pray, I thought. *Surely I have to do something!*

Just pray.

I was learning to trust God as our provider. If I could provide for the ministry through my own efforts and talents, I'd never know if it was God or me making it happen.

But when a disconnect notice arrived for non-payment of the ministry phone bill, I was upset. If we didn't pay $400 by Monday at 5 p.m., our phones would be turned off. God had my attention! Desperate for an answer, I went away to a retreat center where I could fast and pray for the night.

Repenting there before the Lord, He began to show me areas of my heart . . . times when I'd clearly exhibited wrong attitudes toward my husband. "Lord, forgive me," I desperately prayed. Finally feeling a spiritual release, I went home.

Sunday afternoon the doorbell rang. Marc, a Vietnam vet we had ministered to occasionally, and who often struggled with unemployment, stood at the door.

"I don't know why," he said, "but the Lord told me to empty out my savings account and give you this money." He then handed Chuck exactly four hundred dollars.

We wept and thanked God together.

The next five years were filled with adventures in faith as God provided for our family. We didn't always have what we wanted, but we always ate (sometimes out of the food bank), and we were learning to trust God.

While learning to trust, I hadn't yielded all areas of my life to the Lord. As I threw myself into the ministry work with the same intensity I put into my business, soon the ministry became as much of an idol as striving for money and success in business.

We worked six days a week, and sometimes seven, for five years without taking a break. Sundays we'd often speak in churches, so our boys didn't see much of us. After work, phone calls would have us meeting the needs of those who were hurting.

Watchman Nee refers to the "wearing down tactics of Satan." I had allowed people and circumstances to wear me down to the point where I was totally operating in the flesh—depending on my own strength—over the last year we were involved in the ministry.

One morning in 1991 at the annual Point Man campout, I felt the Lord giving me some direction as I was journaling my prayers. I sensed God was leading me into a ministry of restoration in the body of Christ. He had already done so much restoration in my life, including healing my heart from the aftermath of my abortion years before.

Now I felt I was to sit at His feet and learn to be sensitive to His voice. That would be the only way I would stay on track and know the difference between a good idea and a God idea.

A month later something happened that changed the course of my life.

And not for the better.

A woman at church "felt led" to give me a bottle of herbs concocted by a naturopath to help me lose weight without diet and exercise. The herbs were purported to be a healthy herbal weight-loss alternative with added benefits to help others take their healthcare into their own hands.

"If you like what this does for you and want to sell the product, I'll help you," she said. When I took the herbal mixture, I felt my body bursting with energy and my mind racing. It didn't hurt that my extra weight dropped off as I continued on the supplements.

Yes! I thought. Helping people find the source of their problems, rather than trying to get rid of the symptoms with medication, had been a passion of mine for years. And then there was the potential financial benefit. I thought about all the good I could do with the extra money if I sold the product.

We were a non-profit ministry, and we needed funds to build up the network around the country. *I could fund the printing and distribution of the free newspaper for vets. I could help underwrite a building project at church. We can take on a few more missionaries to support.*

I was quick to seize the opportunity to be a distributor for this new multi-level marketing (MLM) business. I was back in business! Denial ruled, and greed kicked in. I felt so good taking the product that I didn't even ask the Lord if I should get involved. It just *seemed* right, so I went for it. After five years without a dependable income, I was ready to make some money.

I had totally forgotten how the same business model had created an unhealthy idolatry in my life with A.L. Williams. My direction to listen to God's voice and be involved in a ministry of restoration became a distant memory as my wheels began turning. I jumped in with both feet, not realizing I was swallowing the first multi-level marketing (MLM) lie: "The ends justify the means."

Multi-level marketing and I were made for each other. My gifts of communication and persuasion easily rallied the troops as I built my organization. It was easy for me to use my influence and enthusiasm to recruit "downline" in the church. My goal was to find or create relationships with those who had influence in the church. First, I'd ask for their help in referring me to others who might need what I had. Pastors and their wives, and anyone involved in ministry were ideal targets.

I'd say, "So many other people in the ministry are involved. It's a great way to fund new projects and help with ministry expenses. You'll be able to build your business fast as there'll be so many people who'll want to help you."

It wasn't long before I became a top producer, with my personal income up to $21,000 a month! *A month!* I had built a huge organization, opened a product distribution center with other distributors coming in as shareholders, and been active on Christian radio touting the product.

But then it all came crashing down. The company's herbal formula was outed as being destructive, and the business practices of the company began undercutting the distributors' commissions. Finally, the distribution center was not making enough money to meet the monthly overhead.

In the months to follow, it was clear to me I had made a terrible mistake in judgment . . . and had led others into a company with unethical leadership and products that were not entirely safe. But multi-level marketing had been so good to me that I didn't want to give up. I found another MLM company with a new high-end product—hardware this time—and encouraged my distributors to follow me.

But God was working on me. He had His ways to get my attention. He began to show me how I had been using my God-given ability to inspire and motivate people for the wrong ends. I was using this gift to make money and build a successful business, rather than inspiring others to walk closer with Jesus. I began to feel a powerful conviction for what I had done over the past three years. I had been rebellious, disobedient, and downright sinful.

The pendulum had swung on the vow I had made when I was nineteen not to let anyone "use" me. I had become the user. In my quiet moments, the Lord revealed to me how I had been using others, as they had been using me. I had used the shareholders to make myself look good and make money. They used me and my leadership talents to make money.

I was acting as if I had to control every situation at all costs. I didn't allow myself to become vulnerable to others. People couldn't be trusted, so I had to make sure I never got hurt again.

I had a choice to make. I knew I had to draw a boundary and say, "No more. I won't be leading you into the promised land. I won't play the same role."

The result was hard feelings all around; investors had lost their financial investment, and I lost friends.

My successful ways of doing business—my standard operating procedure—that had made us thousands upon thousands of dollars was a dream circling the drain into failure.

There was no going back. "Lord, help me! I never want anything in my life that is not Your will."

I had lived my life with one good idea after another. Many had paid off. But, just because they made money, were they necessarily God's ideas for my life? Just because a door opened, did that mean I was supposed to walk through it?

I hadn't asked the Lord in prayer or had godly counsel on whether I should jump back into MLM. I hadn't waited for peace and confirmation. Because of that, I set myself up to be wide open to deception.

Those three years of disobedience almost cost me my marriage, my spiritual life, and my integrity. Chuck had walked away from his calling to minister to Vietnam veterans a year after I had disobediently jumped back into the business world. He had been carrying the burden of the ministry alone and was burned out. He could have used my administrative help, but I was just too busy doing "my thing" to notice he needed me. I had become self-centered again to the point of being blind to the needs of my husband and family.

When the enormity of the mess I had made hit me, I fell into depression. I retreated to my house, didn't take phone calls, and didn't even get dressed most days. I could no longer promote this "road to success" but didn't know how to deal with the fallout or what would be next. *How will we live?*

When I couldn't even pray for myself, God would send a friend by the house, and she'd pray for me. Gradually, as I turned my face to the Lord, slowly, slowly, I began to gain strength and call out to God myself.

"Oh God! Cause me to hate the things You hate and love the things You love!"

"I want to be excited about Your kingdom, not worldly projects and ventures."

"Help me to value relationships and people for what and who they are, not for what I can get out of them."

"Remove the strongholds in my life that cause me to love the things of this world more than You."

One August afternoon, I lay on my bed and sobbed uncontrollably for hours. I wailed at the top of my lungs with a soul pain so intense I could hardly stand it. When it was over, I felt different. Something lodged in my being had been removed, stripped out. In its place was a peace, a fulfillment, a true longing for the things of God. I felt transformed by the power of the Holy Spirit.

I was hearing God's voice again. God had done a new work in me and I was amazed.

FIVE

Writing the Next Chapter

Let love and faithfulness never leave you; bind them around your neck, write them on the tablet of your heart.

—Proverbs 3:3

As Chuck and I prayed and fasted, we asked God, "Lord, show us what to do to pay our bills." We felt strongly He wanted us to work *together* as a couple. No more "lone ranger" stuff.

Chuck had picked up the slack during my three months of darkness by rustling up photography and book publishing jobs. We had barely kept up with our house payments on our home overlooking the waters of Puget Sound each month as my income dwindled away.

During the early days of Point Man we had developed a book as a resource for the ministry but couldn't find a traditional, royalty publisher for the project as we weren't famous enough to justify taking a risk on us. After working with an editor who acted as a book packager and helped us rewrite the manuscript, we had the cover designed, the text formatted, got the ISBN number, and the work copyrighted. Then we had 10,000 copies of *Nam Vet: Making Peace with Your Past* printed at a cost of one dollar each. In less than two years, we had sold all the copies.

When an agent approached us to take it to the next level by pitching it to a traditional publisher, we went for it. Multnomah Publishers bought the rights in 1988 and sold 40,000 copies before allowing us to buy the rights back. To date, the book has sold over 250,000 copies and helped untold thousands of Vietnam veterans and their families. Including the copies veteran's organizations have been allowed to print free, there are over a million copies in print.

As our successful self-publishing experience brought inquiries from people asking if we could help them do what we had done with our book, a publishing house—WinePress Publishing—was birthed. We felt impressed we should focus on the publishing business together, working only with Christian writers. We already had published twelve books or so over the previous seven years, some while in the ministry, and had helped friends publish their books on the side. We established rates that were 25–50 percent lower than the competition. We could do it from home, be there for our family, and still serve the body of Christ by offering affordable and professional publishing services. I wouldn't get consumed, and we would be instrumental in touching people's lives.

Little by little, manuscript by manuscript, we began to see the faithfulness of God to bring us enough publishing jobs to pay the bills. We didn't promote, just put the word out and the Lord led people to us. We turned away manuscripts that would bring dishonor to the Lord, even if we needed the money. Our little company became the pioneer of the independent publishing movement in the Christian market and was the first publishing house to offer these kinds of services.

When we began our work with Point Man Ministries, I had only been a believer for six months. I didn't have a solid foundation in the Word. Jesus had radically changed my life, but I hadn't progressed in my knowledge of the Scriptures. Sure, I would read the Word, but I didn't spend quality time with the Lord and would skim over Scriptures in Christian books to get to the authors' words. Even after I began to minister to women who had gone through their own trauma and wounds, telling them they needed to get healing for the wounds that were controlling them, I hadn't done that myself. I didn't realize while ministering to others, my wounds could become my own idols. I was not aware how my own idolatry could leave me open to deception.

During my time working with the ministry, I was asked to speak at many veteran's events over the years. For one of my workshop sessions, I needed to know about some of the enemy warfare tactics the Communist forces used against us in Vietnam. Chuck told me how the Viet Cong (VC) primarily used guerilla warfare because they were outgunned and technologically disadvantaged.

He said, "Hit-and-run tactics and small unit actions were designed to wear us down and to catch us off guard. They avoided direct contact—conventional combat—as much as possible."

The parallels were obvious to me. The enemy of our souls has been outgunned by Jesus and is at a disadvantage. So he uses other tactics to make us ineffective.

As Chuck and I made a list of some of the methods the VC and North Vietnamese soldiers used, we saw an uncanny similarity to methods

Satan uses against believers. We shared this knowledge with the body of Christ through the book *Behind Enemy Lines: A Field Manual for God's Army*.

The comparisons were stunning.

The VC attempted to look as much like the civilian population as possible.

Satan disguises himself and can even appear like a friend—an angel of light.

The VC did not fight only for physical territory; they fought to win the hearts and minds of people.

If Satan can shift our attention, our zeal, our time, our hearts and our minds onto something other than Jesus and the Great Commission, he has won, and we will be unfruitful and ineffective in the Kingdom of God.

The VC deployed booby traps along the trails. This destroyed the confidence of our troops who experienced casualties, but rarely spotted the enemy, while the enemy watched the destruction from afar.

Satan knows he cannot win the war, but if he can set enough traps along our walk to injure us and make us unsure of our faith, he can discourage us.

The VC used innocent civilians, even destroying them as decoys, to undermine security and confidence. Chuck said, "They would strap explosive charges on small children and send them into groups of G.I.s to make friends. When the kids got close enough, they'd detonate the explosives remotely."

Satan will use even seemingly good things to win our affections. Once he has accomplished this, he ambushes us and attempts to destroy us.

The VC had a strategy to get our soldiers to attack their own. "It's called 'cutting the pie,'" Chuck said.

At night the troops would dig into night-defensive positions with the entire unit forming into a large circle (pie) for protection. Normally there were two men to a hole; one slept while the other kept watch, pointing his weapon out into the darkness with his back to the center of the circle.

"The VC would probe a point in the circle, and make a lot of noise to attract attention, and try to take out a slice out of the 'pie.' After penetrating the perimeter in the darkness, they would quickly move back out and off into the night," Chuck said. "Guys on both sides of the circle would hear the same noise inside the circle and end up shooting each other."

Satan deploys the same strategy against us. He creeps into our mindsets and causes disruptive "noise," and then pulls back and waits for us to attack each other. He tries his best to cause fights, quarrels, hurt feelings, bitterness, unmet expectations, dissatisfaction, and dissension, without being detected in marriages, families, churches, and businesses. The Word of God says our battle is not with flesh and blood; if we forget that, the enemy wins.

The VC tried to stay close to U.S. military units. They knew the closer they could be to our troops—especially in a firefight—the less likely it was that our forces would call in artillery or air support for fear of directing the incoming fire on themselves.

Satan, through his minions, gets as close to us as possible, whispering lies and confusing us, so we cannot determine what area to target for "air support."

By sharing Satan's tactics of spiritual warfare, we had begun an important conversation about understanding the strategies of the evil one to successfully fight the battle we are in.

We had also created a huge target on our backs.

I had no idea how vulnerable I was.

Not long after publishing those insights in 1998, something had started to shift in me. I had begun to feel dead inside. I felt as if my life was a sham. I had no victory. I felt no love at all for my husband. I could not find my way back to a place of hope.

I moved into the bedroom downstairs until something changed. I felt like a hypocrite, calling myself a Christian, helping many authors publish their God-given messages, watching my children all grow in Christ and have vibrant relationships with Him, but I could not feel, could not grow, could not find a place of peace. Something was terribly wrong, but I could not figure out what it was. I just knew things were not right inside me.

We tried couple's counseling. The counselor's simple answer was, "Let's think of your marriage as your backyard. You like to play in your backyard—by working. And Chuck likes to play in his backyard, by playing." While giving us a meaningful look, he said, "You need to learn to play in each other's backyards."

One hundred and fifty dollars an hour for that? I thought.

Before this, I had gone to counseling on my own to try to make sense of the blank I drew when I tried to recall the early years of my life. But, when I did not see immediate results, I quit going. Once again, I was crying out for affirmation and not getting it. I was restless for more, but not finding that "more."

Easily distracted, I was swept up into a new "cause"—the potential worldwide disaster the year 2000 changeover—the new millennium—was going to make. With this new cause came the excitement and adrenaline high I craved. I left the search for healing for myself and my marriage, and jumped onboard.

A respectable pastor, who we had published a book for, convinced us and a group of Vietnam veterans and their wives, that we should move to a remote location to prepare to minister to those who would be homeless and helpless after Y2K. After scouting various areas, we decided to move southeast down to Enumclaw, a sixty-minute drive from Seattle. From this more rural setting we would be better placed to offer hope and help to others during the coming disruption.

We were acting out of fear when we bought into the hype that the world as we knew it was going to end. The fear was generated by media reports and exaggerated fears that computers would cease to function and all computerized systems would be in disarray.

I've learned that fear can leave an opening in our lives for the enemy to work. Had I known better what the Word said, or the Father's heart, I wouldn't have been taken in by the pastor's cause of stockpiling food supplies and fearing the future. God said, "Never will I leave you; never will I forsake you" (Heb. 13:5). He promises to help us when we run into problems and trials (Rom. 5:3). We can do all things through Christ, the one who gives us strength (Phil. 4: 13).

We settled in isolation on a property we felt was chosen by God for us. Our daughter gasped as we turned into a driveway displaying a "FOR SALE" sign at the entrance. "This is it! I saw this place in a dream the other night! I believe God is saying this is *Providence,* and He will use it for His glory!" We took as confirmation this was where the Lord wanted us to minister to people and were strengthened in our sense that we were moving in the right direction after our ministry friends, Dennis and Gloria, bought the property.

In Enumclaw, away from our previous stable church relationships and wise counselors, we became more deeply involved with the house church movement that was making its presence felt among the body of Christ at that time. Being in on a cutting-edge movement appealed to my spiritual pride and fed my need to be unique, special, and "in the know." The new house church movement was touted as the only "true" church. The teaching we heard was hyper-critical and condemning of the traditional church. As we became connected with ministers in the movement, several pastors with messages that denounced the church came to WinePress with books to be published. They flattered me into believing I was hearing from God when I published their work and touted what a difference doing so would make in the lives of others.

One such man was a house church leader from Greenwater, just east of Enumclaw, whose ministry we were under from 1998–1999. He could quote a lot of Scripture to prove his points, and I was easily convinced. But he eventually controlled, manipulated, and spiritually abused a flock of about seventy in the Enumclaw area. He used Scripture out of context, required us to harshly judge other believers, even family members, and cut them off if they didn't line up with his particular interpretations of Scripture.

He denounced the traditional church in America as having the traits of biblical Babylon. Of course, the truth was known only to him and the others who had jumped on the house church "train." He would often preach on the spirit of Jezebel and how it had infiltrated the church. Anyone who did not agree with him on anything was accused of being controlled by that spirit, usually the women in the church. Those who just wanted to love God and serve him wholeheartedly were being shamed and shunned if they didn't fall into line.

When our daughter did not follow his advice, he called her out as a Jezebel, and we were told to have nothing to do with her.

As the bookkeeper for the house church, I began to see the discrepancies between what he said publicly he was being paid and what he was actually being paid, especially after he demanded everyone increase their tithe. When I confronted him, he screamed at me saying, "You're lying!"

I took two witnesses back with me to address the issue again, and he continued to lash out at us. After I sent proof to the members, the church disintegrated; a few continued to believe his lies, but the rest of the sheep were scattered.

You'd think we would be longing for a message of grace and love after that. Our hearts were set to wholeheartedly serve God, but without wise counsel, and in our pulling away to isolation, we were merely softened up for the next big whammy.

SIX

Into Deception

The thief comes only to steal and kill and destroy . . .

—John 10:10

Remember my decision when I was nineteen—that vow that I would never allow anyone to use me again? Well, Matthew 7:1–2 says, "Do not judge, or you too will be judged. For in the same way you judge others, you will be judged, and with the measure you use, it will be measured to you."

The enemy used my hunger for God with my typical reckless abandon (normal for a type-A) to draw me into what I finally realized was a bona-fide Christian cult. That hunger for God was misused by a man I allowed to become a spiritual authority in my life. He misused that authority and through him, the enemy robbed me of my marriage, my family relationships, my house, car, credit rating, my 3.5-million-dollar Christian publishing company, and almost my faith.

The second pastor in this downward spiral was Tim Williams, founding "pastor" of Sound Doctrine, a wolf in sheep's clothing who spent twelve years using me up and spitting me out. This was the man whom the enemy used to hijack WinePress Publishing and emotionally, financially, relationally, and spiritually bankrupt me over the following twelve years.

Here's how it happened.

I met his wife, Carla, the co-director of a well-known Christian writer's conference in 1996, where I was representing WinePress. I was immediately drawn in by her personal warmth and friendliness and saw her as someone who was deep spiritually and serious about her faith.

When Carla said her "pastor" husband had an edgy manuscript that would convict "wide-road Christians" to follow the narrow road that Jesus demanded, I was intrigued. That desire to have the inside track, an evidence of spiritual pride that had led me into Scientology and then to the house-church mentality, now led me down a road to ruin.

I can't say I wasn't warned. One of our editors reviewed the book Tim Williams had written and wanted us to publish, which he titled *Hating for Jesus*, based on his interpretation of Luke 14:26. The editor strongly warned me saying, "This will promote a destructive message that will be harmful to the body of Christ."

I didn't want to hear that evaluation. My eyes were looking at the bottom line. Williams wanted to print a large quantity of books, so the publishing project would be good for our finances.

This must be the Lord's provision. We had $20,000 of bills that needed to be paid. Instead of listening to sound advice and trusting God to provide some other way, I deceived myself.

"The red flags are just sour grapes," I told Chuck. "The enemy must be trying to get in the way of the Lord's provision. Satan must be trying to keep Tim's challenge to the body of Christ silent."

Nothing could have been farther from the truth. Later, I was to recall the message of Psalms 106:15 (NKJV), "And He gave them their request, but sent leanness into their soul."

We were in a financial bind, but instead of trusting God to provide in a way that did not compromise His Word, I grabbed on to the easy solution and pushed this manuscript to publication in 1998. Without realizing it, by refusing to trust God for our provision, I opened myself up and put my trust in a false prophet and his wife, who led me into a spiritual wasteland that would practically destroy me. My unhealthy longing for the approval and significance only God could give was exploited by those with agendas driven by power, greed and personal gain.

Of course, I didn't know at the outset that Tim Williams would later become the one used by the enemy to hijack and steal WinePress Publishing. He would eventually manipulate and control me, browbeating by using Scripture out of context, and cause great harm to my family. Williams was extremely effective at using Scripture to manipulate, shame and shun believers to obey his "cause for righteousness" (legalism) and give up everything for it. Instead of walking in freedom, the ones who followed him became "burdened again by a yoke of slavery" (Gal. 5:1).

Williams profited personally from the misguided generosity of those seeking to please God. Other former Sound Doctrine members tell their own sad stories of destruction. The number of divorces and broken families in the Williams' wake is tragic. The worst part is many of those who have left the Sound Doctrine cult have completely lost their faith and have ended up spiritually shipwrecked. Many still feel completely intimidated into not telling their stories for fear of repercussions from Williams and his Sound Doctrine lawyer.

I've been asked, "How is it someone as bright and strong and capable as you could be sucked into a cult like Sound Doctrine?"

It just makes no rational sense. Over these years, I was brainwashed little by little into thinking anything done to benefit the Williams family and Sound Doctrine would be honoring to God, so I justified many things I would never have allowed under normal circumstances. I've also concluded the Sound Doctrine agenda was inspired and driven by unholy spirits so there was a level of deception/blindness that I believe was demonic.

We were taken in by Tim Williams' passion. His book, *Hating for Jesus*, was edgy, but filled with a new look at Scripture that demanded true Christians would walk as Jesus walked. He set out to prove that if you "hate for Jesus," you are loving God with all your heart. When you "hate for Jesus," you do whatever Tim says God wants you to do, no matter what your spouse, kids, parents, or friends think or say.

Desperate to fill a need in my life, this righteous zeal seemed to be an answer to my prayers. Of course, I wanted to love God with everything!

We invited the Williams family to come to Enumclaw for a time of fellowship in late July. While they were here, Chuck invited them to move to Enumclaw to start a church. The date was set for them to move in early September 1999. When Tim said he didn't believe those in ministry should own a home, we bought a house in Enumclaw for them to live in rent free. The only way I could qualify for the loan was to say I would be living there—that it would be an owner-occupied loan—even though that was a lie. Tim allowed this since I was doing it "for the Lord."

That was the first red flag I ignored but certainly not the last.

It wasn't long before the indoctrination began.

If anyone questioned his authority or the way he used Scripture, Tim accused them of lying and being in sin. It was always someone else who was haughty, arrogant, and prideful.

Titus 2:4–5 was overemphasized, as well as 1 Timothy 2:11–13, dealing with the behavior of women. I had been a water-baptized active Christian for fifteen years and had spent years in full-time ministry, but I was told that I really was not a Christian because I did not "hate for Jesus."

"Throw out everything you think you know and start with a clean slate," Tim Williams taught. He would quote 1 Corinthians 1:18 out of context, "For the message of the cross is foolishness to those who are perishing, but to us who are being saved it is the power of God." He boldly proclaimed only *his* message was truth, and only those who embraced his message are being saved and will have the power of God.

Maybe I never had a pure heart. Maybe I was never truly born again. I asked to be re-baptized.

It's convicting to look back and see how the enemy worked through Tim and how gullible I was. The first sermon tape we listened to was entitled "Praise God for Y2K." Instead of the normal fearmongering most were perpetuating on the topic, Tim said all Christians would suffer in the end times, and we should rejoice that Y2K could be the time when we would be tested and could prove our love for Jesus by embracing the storm instead of trying to prepare to endure it. The closer January 1, 2000 approached, the more Tim declared it was not going to be the issue everyone was convinced it would be. This insight, perhaps provided by the unholy realm, just gave Tim Williams more credibility when the clock struck midnight and nothing happened.

The repercussions in our family didn't take long to occur. Early on, my youngest son, Aaron, and Chuck's son, Ailen, joined the church.

My son Garrett, who worked at WinePress and had been recently married, seemed open to helping us start the church, but his wife and in-laws, wisely, did not agree. When Tim decided he did not "do God's will" by "hating" his wife, we were told to cut him off and no longer associate with him. We were instructed by Tim to go to Garrett's house and fire him from his job with WinePress since he would not repent but was allowing his wife to be his idol.

Then when Roby did not agree to come and help us build the new church, she too was rebuked for being in sin by marrying her husband as she was a divorced woman. She was cut off and we were directed not to speak to her again. We were told we had to "stand against" our family members' "sin" in hopes they would repent someday.

Four months into the church plant, Chuck was through with it. After experiencing the rage of Tim Williams in a heated conversation, he came to me and said, "I'm not leaving you; I'm leaving the church." He resigned from the church and tried to talk me out of publishing any more of Tim's books. One book was ready to go to the printer at the time. By then, Tim's books were being published at WinePress's expense instead of him having to pay for them like everyone else. When Chuck tried to stop the book from going to press, this was viewed as sabotage of "the Lord's work."

Chuck was now the enemy and had to be destroyed.

After Chuck reached out by e-mail to many in the publishing industry and all our friends and family, saying I was in a "hating cult," articles ran in national publications, *Christian Retailing* (front-page story "WinePress Publishing Marriage Turns to Sour Grapes") and *Charisma* ("Hating for Jesus Draws Controversy").

Tim called this all persecution and slander and gossip and used Scripture to push his agenda. He advised me to divorce Chuck, citing 1 Corinthians 7:15 about allowing the "unbeliever" to leave.

Since Chuck only worked at WinePress about ten hours a week, and I worked full-time, I was told, "The business should be yours. You don't have to give him anything for it."

After trying for months to negotiate some sort of settlement for the business, and us not giving an inch, Chuck finally walked away.

Tim and Carla poured evil suspicions into my head by telling me, "He's probably been cheating on you all along." I knew this was not true, but my heart was easily turned away from him as I had labeled him the enemy.

Months before the divorce, he ended up on his daughter's couch with no car, no money, no job, no possessions. He waited and hoped for me to leave the cult. After our divorce was final six months later, he married an old girlfriend.

Tim Williams began counseling me on how to run my million-dollar-a-year business and gave me "pastoral advice" on how to make it a "godly business." We began giving 7 percent of the gross income to the church. WinePress was now the official cash cow of Sound Doctrine church. The church opened a Christian bookstore in town, the Salt Shaker, financed by the money given to the church by WinePress. All non-church members were let go from WinePress Publishing so only Sound Doctrine church members were employed there.

Six months into the church plant, a WinePress author challenged me on Tim's theology. What he said made sense, and I tried to talk to Carla and others on the way home from a conference in Spokane. My cell phone got bumped during the conversation and inadvertently called Tim's phone number, and he heard the entire conversation. I was rebuked for not setting the author straight and being a people pleaser. I was now a Saul, a Judas, a betrayer, could not be trusted, and had to be watched.

About a year into the church plant, my youngest son, Aaron, decided to leave. Because he didn't just go away but tried to stay in touch with me, as well as staying in touch with Chuck, they labeled him a troublemaker and divisive. They advised me not to have anything to do with him, justifying it with Scripture. Aaron continued over the next eleven years to call and write me letters; most all of them were intercepted by WinePress/church leadership, and I never knew about them. Tim also decided to send a restraining order to Aaron to keep him away from WinePress, which I knew nothing about.

Members were encouraged to live like the early church with "all things in common." Jan, a woman who divorced her husband and came up from California to join the church, gave over half a million dollars from the sale of her house to the church after being told she "didn't have the wisdom to know how to spend money."

Tim and his wife, Carla, targeted those with disabilities who were developmentally disabled in some way, and of course, those who were so broken from childhood abuse, vulnerable souls, who were easily manipulated and controlled for a variety of reasons.

Around this time, my father passed away. With my new holier-than-thou attitude, I told my mom and brothers, "I won't be attending the memorial service." (I told myself this was best because I'd have to tell them my dad wasn't going to heaven because he didn't hate for Jesus). Instead, I sent a card to my mom quoting the Scripture "Let the dead bury the dead," the standard "hating your mother and father" Scripture to use in a situation like this.

Sometime in 2001, while I was away representing the company at a writers' conference, Tim had my son and some of the other guys build a large bonfire at a church member's property and burn all the copies of my books since they were written before the hating for Jesus message and were therefore deemed worthless. I learned about this much later. About 1,000 copies of *Consumed by Success* were burned after 6,000 copies had been sold. *All That Glitters is Not God* was newer; I had printed 5,000 and only sold about 1,000 when they were burned.

When I found out, I felt as if I had been robbed . . . as if my house had been ransacked. I felt slimed. How could everything God had shown me in the past have been wrong? Emotionally beaten down with constant verbal and written criticism, I didn't speak out but kept my feelings to myself. But a part of me died inside as I wondered if the message God had given me and I had written in those books in obedience, was a lie.

By early 2002, the business was having financial problems mostly because of all the money we were giving to the church. At this time, we started a Print on Demand (POD) division, and finances eventually improved.

I watched as greed seemed to get a hold of Tim Williams and his wife and family, another red flag I ignored. Over the next years every inch of his house was updated. Of course, no one dared question him why, suddenly, Scripture now permitted a pastor to own a home, when before it said he shouldn't. That was the basis for us buying the house for the Williams to live in rent-free when they came. The hypocrisy I let slide was criminal. But every time I pointed out something wrong, it was turned back on me as the one needing to repent. I began to shrivel up and die inside and stopped speaking the truth in love.

All supplies were charged on the ministry Home Depot card and paid for by the ministry, even though the house was owned personally by Tim Williams. He bought the latest gadgets, the newest and best computers, the best in clothes and office décor. When he'd give away his leftovers, Carla praised him for being so generous.

Although I had always been in charge of the company, because I was a woman, Tim had a long-range plan to phase me out. He wanted me to only work part time so I'd fit in with his godly-woman description from 2 Timothy 2:11.

As Tim had more and more involvement in the business, the church changed their articles of incorporation to include "business consulting" to their activities. The amounts of money given to Sound Doctrine by WinePress as business consulting fees were then nearing a quarter million a year.

When my stepson, Ailen, left the church in November of 2004, his wife, who stayed in Sound Doctrine, was counseled to divorce him and do everything possible to see he never got the kids.

Shortly after, Tim and Carla began zeroing in on the kids in the church, becoming "Grandpappy and Granny" to them. I was replaced as Grandmama to my grandkids, Anna and Ezekiel, as were other parents and grandparents whose roles were also minimized with their children and grandchildren. We were also encouraged to call Tim and Carla "Dad and Mom" since they were our spiritual parents.

Tim controlled our salaries, who could drive, who would make which house payments, all based on who was deemed to be in a repentant state at the time.

The fallout was deep and wide. Using Scripture out of context, Tim Williams regularly sowed discord in families; he turned wives against husbands, husbands against wives, children against their parents, adult children against their parents, all to gain control. He intentionally would keep one or two marriages together just to be able to point to them to say he wasn't destroying families. He used Luke 14:26 to divide families so those under his care were easier to control for his own benefit.

Five years of brainwashing was complete by mid-2005. I had been brought along to the conclusion that the right thing to do was for me to give up ownership of WinePress if I wanted to do God's will. The business was becoming more and more successful. Since I was so "prideful" and full of "selfish ambition," I couldn't handle the success, spiritually. Tim decided I should "sell" the business to him. But, of course, he wouldn't pay me for it, since I was greedy and wouldn't have a pure heart if I was going to gain anything from giving up WinePress.

He began gearing up to step into the publishing executive and business owner roles. He retired from ministry to run WinePress and promoted his two sons (Joshua and Josiah) and Malcolm Fraser into leadership of the church.

Before selling the publishing company to Tim Williams, I confessed having thoughts of firing everyone at WinePress and hiring people from local churches. My confession incited the wrath of Tim Williams, and I had to be punished for my "sin." I was again labeled a Judas. In a public meeting in my living room, I was put in a chair in the middle of a circle, and the church members took turns declaring their hatred for me for more than an hour. I was told, "You are hindering God's will for the company." I was told I was a selfish boss, and that Tim Williams should be in charge as, "he is godly, and you aren't."

Thoroughly shamed and punished for my thoughts, with the church turned against me, I acquiesced. What could have been deliverance for the company was hijacked once again.

As discipline, Tim decided to "punish" me by not buying WinePress from me. He marched into my office and said something to the effect of, "I will not play second fiddle to you. I'm in charge even if I'm not the owner. You will pay me $250,000 a year, and you have no say in how the company is run. You are unfit to hear from God as to what is best for WinePress."

Tim Williams was now running WinePress as if it were his own and making all the financial decisions, instead of just being a consultant. He brought over all the full-time volunteers from the church bookstore and ministry and hired them at WinePress, and instituted a bizarre "No Gossip Policy" to control what authors said about WinePress. I could no longer decide or question how money was spent. Malcolm Fraser, the assistant pastor of the church, was the executive officer at WinePress and was Tim's right-hand man.

Tim began to systematically replace me in all areas of my authority with his wife, Carla. He controlled what I did and said and eventually ordered me to quit my leadership roles in the Northwest Christian Writers Association, the Enumclaw Downtown Partnership, and Enumclaw Rotary.

Tim bought a second house, his wife started flying first class, he set salaries for his two sons at $100,000+. Joshua was now being paid $100,000+ by WinePress, but worked full time at the church-owned Salt Shaker bookstore in downtown Enumclaw. Joshua and Josiah Williams, and other staff members, bought houses with no money down, qualifying for loans by showing higher incomes than they had. Cooking the books, I later learned, had become the order of the day. His sons were given raises for a few paychecks to be able to qualify for loans they were not qualified for.

The Williams family was being paid close to $500,000 a year combined, while office and warehouse rent was paid late, printer bills were ignored, and editors were forced to wait for months on end, but Tim was never to be paid late. Most of the rest of the staff worked for minimum wages to "bless" the ministry of the Williams family, or for some of the divorced men in the church, to prove income was so low alimony or child support could only be paid in the minimum amount.

Tim raised the prices on WinePress services and kept raising them to the point where they were no longer competitive. I struggled over them using lawyers and threatening to sue anytime anyone ever crossed them, the exorbitant service charges for filling orders on print-on-demand books, and for never being willing to commit to publication dates. They'd sell prospects on being better than royalty publishers, but when authors complained, would then remind them they were self-publishing.

WinePress was always right, and the authors were wrong. If an author complained, no apology would be given, but the author would be intimidated into apologizing for complaining.

I got in trouble many times for taking authors' sides in a conflict. This was so far out of the bounds of how I wanted to treat customers, it made me cringe.

Ridiculed and humiliated, I was told, "You are in sin and need to repent," whenever I disagreed with Tim Williams, which was frequently. He used my invitations to speak at writers' conferences as a tool to control me. If I didn't behave the way he expected, the privilege was taken from me.

All the control and berating was portrayed as the Lord's discipline. I was told the Lord loves those He disciplines, so I must learn to embrace "the cross" and rejoice in the discipline God was pouring out upon me. As is typical in cults, shaming and shunning were the key control techniques.

The brainwashing came in many forms. Tim would preach on dying to self, pointing out our besetting sins. He controlled through asking others in the group to confront individuals who were deemed in sin and not let up until they saw some "godly sorrow"—tears and the right words in response. Tim's style was to tell someone else how to rebuke you and report back to him to be praised or cursed for how it went.

One time in the WinePress conference room, he went down the line telling each person, "If you don't repent, you are going to hell," but bypassed his two sons, his wife, and his next-in-line, Malcolm.

Once he took over control of WinePress in 2006, he instituted an online message board that all staff were logged into all the time. He used it to rebuke us, call us names, and shame us. A feature programmed into the computer program would lock out the one being shamed. There was no choice but to read his ranting and rambling vitriol and waste hours, and sometimes a whole work day, doing so.

In 2008, WinePress owed $10,000 in taxes. I was told I needed to make arrangements with the IRS to pay the $10,000 by getting a personal loan to pay this tax bill. I did not receive any of the refunds, yet I was to be responsible to pay the taxes.

In 2009, WinePress did 3.5 million in sales, but Tim was out of control on his spending. He began more aggressively moving me out of the spotlight and discrediting me.

Finally, in early March 2010, I was fed up, ready to walk away. I had finally come to terms with being willing to say I must not be a Christian anymore. If this is who God was, I didn't want Him. In a meeting with leadership, Tim wanted me to sign a paper saying they had full control if I was ever incapacitated. Frustrated and defeated, I just said, "Why don't you just take the company?"

What Tim had been working toward was finally within his grasp. He let no grass grow under his feet and had the paperwork immediately drawn up and dated for April 1, 2010. Yes, on April Fool's Day, 2010, the ownership of the company transferred to the new LLC in Sound Doctrine's name. A Letter of Intent had been signed by me saying I would "sell" the company to them for $10. They proceeded to box me into a corner with additional agreements, like a life-time non-compete agreement, a gag-order basically saying I could never say anything negative about WinePress or the "church." Another agreement said they were not buying the liabilities of the company; I was responsible for them, but if I was a "good girl," they would pay them.

In the sale paperwork, they included a letter I penned back in 2006 (at Tim's insistence and direction) declaring I was, of my own free will, selling the company for $10 to Tim Williams because it was God's will and because he had saved the company. In this statement, I also declared it was just their greed talking if my children or anyone else questioned my decision to sell (give) the business. They kept my www.athenadean.com domain name and took all the rights to my book on self-publishing as assets. I never received any royalties on any book sales the entire time the Williams were involved, even though Tim, Carla, and Joshua were always paid their royalties.

Because of the constant shaming, every time I had a negative thought or saw a red flag, I believed it was my sin. I truly felt I was the betrayer, a Judas, and I needed to repent. Over and over I said, "I'm sorry," for being bitter against Tim. I declared if anything bad ever happened to WinePress it was entirely my fault (this having been fed to me over and over by Tim Williams).

For my perceived sins, I was busted down to minimum wage, taken off the front lines, put in the accounting department where I wasn't to talk to anyone, co-workers, or authors. They disabled my e-mail, took the phone off my desk, took my picture off the staff page on the in-house website. I was not even introduced to prospective authors when they came for a tour of WinePress, even though they still used my book *Your Book in Print* (originally *You Can Do It: a Christian Guide to Self-Publishing*) as a sales tool. Little by little, Tim and Carla had me take out helpful content in the book and turn it into a puff piece about the two of them, touting how godly they were and how they had turned WinePress around and changed my life.

The economy had taken a toll on WinePress profits, but unnecessary expenditures had not been cut when sales were down. Bills were overdue, while the Williams family was being paid almost half a million a year and they weren't trying to cut back—still flying first class, not using the Amex points for tickets but paying cash we didn't have, daily business lunches, etc. As I began to see the incriminating evidence while I performed the simple bookkeeping tasks in QuickBooks, I wrote an e-mail to Tim and Malcolm outlining how income was down and questioning why expenses were not being cut.

Rebuked for being a Judas and bitter, I was intimidated into apologizing and repenting for what I said. I was told to shred all my journals and delete all e-mails I had ever sent, including the one to Tim and Malcolm because I was a "witch" and my written and spoken words were "sorcery."

My beat-down sessions continued. I was completely demonized to the rest of the church and alienated from everyone. I had no choice but to look for part-time work because I was told I was responsible for a huge IRS bill as well as the state sales tax.

I was now officially the enemy and could not be trusted. I was berated, ridiculed and humiliated at every turn. Then, as if I couldn't go any lower, I was demoted from the accounting department. Looking back, it's obvious they didn't like the access I had to all the evidence of Tim's out-of-control spending and the damning proof that he always paid himself and his family first while expecting everyone else to wait for what was due to them. I was put on full-time cleaning duty at a minimum wage. On minimum wage, I had no way to pay all the tax liabilities they had convinced me were mine.

I felt about as low as I could possibly go. But my eyes were beginning to be opened to what was actually happening. I finally dared feel indignant at the injustice, the wrongs, and the greed evident in the company and the church.

Amazingly, I still thought my salvation was wrapped up in working at WinePress and being in Tim and Carla's good graces.

After cutting my hours down to two days a week of cleaning toilets and dumping trash, they told me they would accept my resignation thirty days after the taxes were filed, since I'd "already been resigning in my heart all along." They coerced me into writing a statement saying I was responsible for all tax liabilities.

They said I owed $50,000 in capital gains taxes and $15,000 to the State of Washington for the sale of the company. I talked to the state about the taxes, and they tried to tell me it was not my bill to pay but the new company's. They said, if the amount wasn't paid right away, they'd go to the LLC for payment. They suggested I amend my return and make the LLC pay since it was not my responsibility. I was still convinced I was doing this all for God and couldn't bring myself to allow the bill to revert to WinePress.

The beginning of the end came two days later when I received a letter from the WinePress attorney threatening to sue me if I didn't pay the bill right away. Sue *me*? The company Chuck and I had founded and I had been coerced into selling for $10 was threatening to sue me?

I immediately went to my brother Jim to see if I could borrow the money to pay the taxes. I still thought I was doing the right thing, even though I felt like I'd been kicked in the gut by their threat to sue.

Jim's question opened my eyes. "If neither of you researched and found out about the sales tax needing to be paid at the time of the sale, why are you solely responsible for the tax? Why aren't you splitting the responsibility?"

My eyes were opened. It was like, ding, ding, ding, ding . . . I could finally see it. In a moment, I realized I had been duped for the past twelve years. I was done! I resigned from the church by sending a comment on their website, "I quit. Since you already have my house, my car, and my business, I guess you can go ahead and sue me . . . there's nothing left for you to get."

Planning to declare bankruptcy and go away, I figured I could get a job in another industry. At the back of my mind I hoped I wasn't going to hell. We had all been brainwashed to believe those who left the church were turning their back on God, so now I was one of "them."

The bankruptcy attorney I consulted was indignant and said, "You need to sue for damages or to get the company back." A local CPA called it fraud and a sham and encouraged me to fight. I then amended my excise tax return and told the state it was filed in error and the LLC needed to pay it.

I realized I needed a bulldog of an attorney to go after them to at least get rid of the capital gains IRS bill, lift the non-compete, pay my attorney fees, and pay off all my credit card bills (including a loan I took out to pay the WinePress tax bill years earlier). I wanted the rights back to my book, my domain name, and wanted my name taken off their blogs and websites. I no longer supported them and did not want any positive things I'd said over the years used.

I didn't want the company back since they had run it into the ground and ruined its reputation. I just didn't want them to keep on abusing others.

Come hell or high water, I was not afraid of them anymore.

A literary attorney I hired sent two demand letters to them which they basically ignored. I reported the situation to the IRS, the Washington attorney general's office, and an investigative reporter.

I praised God I was free. Regardless of the personal price to my reputation ahead, I started telling my story. My prayer was that those who were left in the cult would have their eyes opened and come out of the deception and bondage they were all under.

The numbers in the group had dwindled by then. There were never many in the church. Over the twelve years I was involved, there were about seventy-five. After I came out, there were about forty people left in the church, including one member in Springfield, Missouri, and one woman and her children in North Carolina. Thirteen of those were children, and eleven were Williams family members. Two of the children were my grandchildren, Anna and Ezekiel. There hadn't been a visitor at a church service in at least two years.

In May of 2013, Malcolm Fraser, the second in line at the Sound Doctrine church was convicted on two counts of first-degree child rape and two counts of first-degree molestation of a child, the daughter of a family in the church, despite the lies of cult members on the witness stand. He was sentenced to eighteen years in prison. Even after being found guilty on all charges, there are still a group of followers convinced Malcolm is innocent. True to form, Malcolm declared he was innocent, and Tim Williams stood by him.

In a way, this was the missing piece of the typical cult behavior, as sexual abuse is often prevalent. The emphasis in Sound Doctrine had been heavy on purity and not even kissing until marriage. But the ongoing shaming that resulted when anyone questioned authority also quietly created an environment where predators could get away with just about anything. Attempts to divert attention from Malcolm Fraser's child rape charges were made in a barrage of articles by Tim Williams online citing cases of false confessions. But the wheels of justice were rolling.

As I look back on how the Sound Doctrine members could declare Malcolm innocent with such passion and be willing to lie on the witness stand in an attempt to see him go free, I can clearly see the way Tim Williams intentionally brainwashed everyone years earlier. Tim started blogging incessantly about the Innocence Project. This is a nonprofit organization representing those who've been falsely accused and convicted of crimes they did not commit due to faulty police investigations and corrupt prosecutors. Then, he ranted on his blog about false memory syndrome. He wrote how you cannot just believe a girl who says she was molested or sexually abused as a child because, in most cases, she is just trying to get attention and is not really a victim. This was all the focus of his blog a good five years before the truth came out.

I believe Malcolm confessed to Tim what he'd done. Rather than exposing the truth and reporting it, Tim proceeded to cover up the crime in a most insidious way.

It's no wonder Sound Doctrine members were appalled when Malcolm was arrested for child rape and did not even ask the question, "Could it be true?" The brainwashing had been so effective, they believed this was just another incident of Satan attacking them through me. I was a person designated as doomed to destruction because of my rebellion and sin. They were told I was the one who convinced the victim to make up this sordid story to try to destroy the "church."

Former members who left the cult in 2013 say Tim is now bunkered in at his place in Ashford that church money turned into a beautiful mountain cabin. Carla died in early October 2013 of a brain tumor. Ridiculously, I was even blamed for this on their hardtruth.us website.

Tim is apparently day trading with the money gleaned through the years from WinePress. The church has closed, but there could be as many as twenty-two adults still loyal to Tim.

But I am not one of them. My eyes are wide open.

Over the years, I ignored many red flags. I questioned when incidents took place that seemed as if God had answered Tim's prayers or given him insight and validated him. *What if Satan is the one orchestrating these things just to keep us all sucked into a lie?* Of course, I rebuked myself for the thought instead of realizing God was trying to open my eyes.

SEVEN

Walking Away

For He has rescued us from the dominion of darkness and brought us into the kingdom of the Son he loves, in whom we have redemption, the forgiveness of sins.

—Colossians 1:13–14

November 10, 2011, I packed my bags and called my son. "Aaron, it's your mom. Where are you? I'm coming." Words I had been convinced would mean I was turning my back on God. But those words were the beginning of my freedom and deliverance.

That phone call was the first step in reconnecting with all the family members who I cut out of my life when they did not agree with Tim Williams.

I had lost my marriage, my relationships with all my kids, my house, my car, and the company. All for believing a con man who knew just how to quote Scripture out of context to control and manipulate those who had zeal without knowledge. A con man who was a master at using shame, condemnation, and the fear of losing salvation to get his followers to do nearly anything to please him for his own selfish, evil gain.

But, oh, how glorious is the grace of God! How He can take destruction and use it for good is beyond me . . . but it is exactly what He has done.

After twelve years, I had lost everything, except my faith. For a time, I considered walking away from what I had believed too, thinking in my heart, *If this is God, then I don't want Him.*

Now I was all but a shell of a person, bruised to near spiritual death. A spiritual, emotional, and financial rape victim, I exhibited all the symptoms of a battered wife. I had been beaten down with the Word of God taken out of context, battered into submission with the threat of the condemnation and judgment of an angry God.

When I came out, I even looked different on the outside.

Before being in the cult, I had long blonde hair and wore unique and attractive styles of clothing. Once sucked into the cult I was maneuvered with Scriptures like the ones about modest clothing and no braided hair, and not wearing jewelry, and women not wearing men's clothing, and selfish ambition, and how sinful it was to draw attention to myself. The application of 1 Corinthians 11:1: "Follow my example, as I follow the example of Christ" had the effect of causing all the women in the group to try to dress and look like Carla with her long dark, undyed hair, jumpers and tennis shoes. We all looked frumpy in our drab colors.

Because I had an income and took Carla shopping, she eventually morphed out of a brown-wren-look into classier and more attractive styles. But since the rest of us were expected to give all our excess income to the church and would be open for criticism if we spent it on ourselves, we all dressed plainly. I stopped having my hair done, and my hair settled into its natural darker color. I no longer spent money on my nails or anything considered selfish. Because I was regularly shamed anytime I wore anything drawing attention to myself, drab-colored clothing was the order of the day. If I wore any colors that made me stand out or look especially attractive, or brought out the blue of my eyes, or made me unique in anyway, it was considered selfish ambition, and I was called out on it.

When I came out, I knew I had been delivered from that deception. But, for a time, I didn't know who I was anymore. I had been told what I should like and dislike and hadn't been free to express my personality and preferences.

Who am I? What do I even like? I questioned. My personality had been submerged until I wasn't sure how I should act, after being shamed for being strong and articulate and confident. It took a while for me to wrap my head around the freedom of being able to choose things I liked, the style of clothing I preferred, and what represented me. Being able to choose what styles and colors and looks I liked in clothes, in decorating, in everything, was liberating.

With no income, I learned to glean at local consignment shops to learn what styles I liked and felt comfortable in. I had to overcome the words in my head: *Don't look too attractive; it won't be pleasing to God.* I didn't go too far the other direction and always made sure I didn't wear low-cut tops or skin-tight skirts or pants. But, as I enjoyed once again shopping to my tastes, I discovered I was drawn to a classic, elegant style, not gaudy or pretentious, but unique and similar to my mom's. My mom always presented herself elegantly in the way she dressed and decorated her home. I never would have thought I'd take after her in any way at all, but this is one area where I did.

I began to choose my own style, from hair and nails and make-up, to clothes, and the way I decorate. I wanted who I am and how I live to glorify God in my unique way. I was learning this was possible, as I allowed God to purify my motives. I was not dressing or doing my hair or decorating my house to compete with others or to portray anything other than reality. I wasn't trying to prove anything or find significance or do anything other than depict the faithfulness of God in my life.

This was a huge difference for me. Before, while I still had so many unexamined issues, I was driven to be important and find significance in what I did, how I looked, and the image I presented. That seemed now like such a distant memory. I felt authentic and where I needed to be. I could put the spotlight on God's faithfulness instead of myself.

After leaving the cult, I began months of intense one-on-one counseling trying to deprogram from all the mind-controlling twisting of Scripture those twelve years had left me with. I wanted to face what draws me to unhealthy, abusive situations like Sound Doctrine. With my warmhearted, kind, professional Christian counselor, I looked at every lie I had believed and then the corresponding truth negating each lie. I examined every faulty, legalistic, and heretical doctrine I'd swallowed hook, line, and sinker. Thankfully, my brother loaned me some money so I didn't have to work for three months and could focus totally on my recovery.

As I went through the healing process, I rediscovered who I was. I learned my personality did not have to die. It has strengths and weaknesses and must be understood in the light of Scripture.

God used my hunger to know Him that led me into spiritual pride and the cult of Sound Doctrine to lead me back to His truth. He showed me how often I called evil good and good evil. My foundation was faulty; I didn't know the difference between Scripture in context and out of context! He showed me how often I quenched the Holy Spirit by quoting Scriptures to Him in error. Yes, I used Scriptures to rebuke the Holy Spirit of God!

If I'd looked above and below the "narrow gate" Scripture, I would have seen two verses that would have stopped me dead in my tracks. The Scriptures warning us to beware of false prophets and those whose fruit was rotten followed the very verse Tim used to reel us in.

Tim never allowed anyone to treat him the way he treated others. He was too arrogant to allow anyone to question him or ask for clarification on the context of a Scripture. And the fruit of his life was bad . . . destructive, hateful, judgmental, condemning, abusive, and void of God's grace and mercy. Yet he portrayed God the Father, Jesus, and the apostle Paul as ones who expected obedience above all. He justified separating families, cutting off friends, and all sorts of abuse by calling it "discipline."

I asked the Lord, *What is wrong with me, that I would believe a lie is the truth for twelve long years and give up everything for it?* This question was a turning point for me and a defining moment in my life, ultimately leading to healing so I could move forward in my life.

Walking away from more than a decade of spiritual abuse and utter devastation brought me to a crossroads. I could become bitter or better. Those were my choices.

Had I looked only at what a train wreck my life was or at all the injustices done to me over my detour into deception, it would have been easy for me to grow bitter. Had I claimed ownership of the "victim" status and focused on everything wrong in my life, I would have naturally blamed it on the cult leader who'd stolen everything from me and left me financially, emotionally and spiritually destitute.

But instead, and only by God's grace, I could ask the hard questions.

"What is my part in this tragedy?"

"Where did I go wrong?"

"What bad choices did I make?"

It's interesting how faulty the human memory becomes over the years. Do we just naturally forget or block out details relating to our own actions and decisions when they've turned out to be bad ones?

After I asked those life-changing questions, friends who were close to me at the beginning of my detour began helping me connect the dots. I needed help to remember how it all began as I had completely blocked from my memory the facts surrounding my decision to rebuff the warnings of others to not get involved with Tim Williams.

Instead, I had plowed ahead, knocking down every red flag waving in my view. Up until November 10, 2011, I kept trying to convince myself I was doing, and had done, God's will. Praise God, He finally allowed the scales to fall from my eyes and gave me the courage to admit how wrong I was. I had believed a lie to be truth for over a decade and had hurt many people who loved me in the process.

After repenting, I began the process of healing and learning who God actually is. He is not an angry taskmaster waiting for me to mess up so I can be disciplined until I repent to His satisfaction. That is a tragically false picture of our loving heavenly Father.

I've learned anew our God is a balance of grace and truth—a loving Father who encourages us to be who He made us to be. In doing so, we glorify Him.

The counselor and I agreed early on that I needed to guard myself against the types of distractions that could easily lead me off the path back to intimacy with Jesus. The three things we determined would be deal breakers in my healing were these: work, a cause, and a man. It seems whenever I'd find myself at a place of despair, when healing needed to come, the enemy always provided a distraction. I was all too happy to run from the pain than to face it, embrace it, and allow Jesus to do His work. But I agreed with my counselor and determined not to distract myself from the pain.

As soon as I did, the enemy tried his best to lead me astray. This set me up to have to go around the mountain one more time before I had another opportunity to find my significance in Christ.

I had been trying to connect with my family of origin and recall more from my growing up years. My little brother had sent me video files of many hours of our growing up footage, including some rare reels of my dad with his mistress and all their holiday celebrations (never on the actual holiday, but later). Before my eyes was the visual proof of my father's double life, the life we knew about but no one saw. Right after I watched the films, I began communicating by Facebook Messenger with a local Christian celebrity of sorts in the Northwest. We had scheduled a time to meet so he could hear my story, hopefully to share on his radio show. Before we did, his real motives became clear when he began to tell me how he'd admired me from afar, and was "excited" to spend time with me. When he asked me not to wear any earrings when we met, and said he was a great masseuse, sirens started to go off.

This was definitely not what I wanted; I was determined to stay far away from his advances. But a part of me was drawn to his stature in the Christian community and "fame" in a number of circles. Never mind that he was married, although currently separated, I was flattered. After I had gotten off the phone with him, a thought popped into my head: *You can still meet him . . . no one has to know. Look how your father lived a double life for the last forty years of his life.*

Before I had a chance to act on the thought, my friend Cindy from Spokane messaged me on Facebook saying, "I don't know what's going on, but you are heavy on my heart. I am praying for you right now!"

I immediately phoned and confessed to Cindy what was going on, including the thought that had popped into my head, and we prayed together. Immediately, by recognizing it, and calling it out, the scheme of the enemy was rendered ineffective and crashed to the ground.

God was protecting me in such amazing ways. It was easy for me to want to make sure my fellowship with Him was not harmed in any way.

The rest of my counseling sessions were productive and life changing. Seeing how I was affected by the lust that influenced my father, and breaking the power of the words spoken over me about having "bedroom eyes" were game changers. I kept my promise to keep from working, joining a cause, or getting involved with a man, and God made great strides in healing my heart.

I began to embrace this truth in my daily life: there is nothing I can do to make God love me more. Trying to do everything right, even repenting just the right way, legalistically doing spiritual disciplines to prove my love for Him, none of those actions would help. They only pushed me away from Him.

I soon came to realize what I had experienced was not of God. Our God is faithful to prove who He *truly* is to us. I am living proof of this fact.

Forty-five days after walking away from the cult I flew down to visit my mom and brother Jim in San Antonio. My mom's Alzheimer's was advanced enough so she didn't remember me. She was pleasant, but what I said didn't seem to register with her.

"Mom," I said, "I'm so sorry I didn't come when Dad died. Can you forgive me?"

She politely listened, but it was as if she was looking at a stranger.

She doesn't remember all the pain I caused her.

Again, I told her how wrong I was and repeated, "Please forgive me."

She finally agreed what I had done was wrong and said, "I forgive you." But I don't think she understood what she was saying.

Had I had come back to Mom too late?

Over the first twelve months of freedom, God tenderly wooed me back to Himself and began restoring:

My relationships with my children;

My sanity and faith in a God of grace and mercy;

My broken, battered and shredded heart;

My desire to love others from the heart rather than keeping them at arm's length;

My love for the body of Christ.

My judgmental and critical spirit was being replaced with one of compassion and mercy;

My homelessness. He gave me a wonderful sanctuary of a house in which to heal and prepare for the next chapter of my life.

EIGHT

Backlash

Have nothing to do with the fruitless deeds of darkness, but rather expose them.

—Ephesians 5:11

While I was beginning to heal, I knew if I told my story, there would be major backlash. But when I walked away, I chose to have nothing more to do with the "fruitless deeds of darkness" perpetrated by Tim Williams and his henchman, Malcolm Fraser, but rather expose them as Ephesians 5:11 instructs.

I was not afraid to tell my story. The Williamses had already gotten everything from me over the twelve years I was deceived, so there was nothing left to get. I was willing to expose those deeds of darkness knowing full well the backlash would be ominous.

The backlash *was* fierce and methodical. Years prior, Sound Doctrine grabbed the Enumclaw.com web address for their rantings and made full use of it after they couldn't sell it to the city for a huge sum. They also continued to threaten to sue me if I didn't pay the $15,000 use tax to the State of Washington. Never mind the technicality that the buyer is required to pay this and not the seller!

After I walked away, I was trying to clear out the house I was living in. The house was leased in my name but filled with Jan Owen's furniture. Mike, Jan's oldest nephew also lived there, as he was tasked with keeping an eye on me for Tim. Jan had been moved to another house in an attempt to keep her from leaving.

Once I left, I sent repeated requests through their attorney to have Mike vacate the house and for Jan to come and get her things. No response. Tim had earlier coerced Mike and Jan to call the landlord and ask him to kick me out of the house and put the lease in their names. He didn't fall for it as he happened to be a friend of mine from Rotary. I did a sale of all my stuff to get rid of it and filled the garage with Jan's furniture. I notified her repeatedly that if she did not take her belongings, I would give them away. The house was finally rented to new tenants, and we were down to the wire. I even contacted Jan's mom in St. Louis, and she was all set to send a truck over to get Jan's stuff. But Jan was not allowed to let her help. I finally went to the police and was assured it would be considered "abandoned property." I could dispose of it however I wanted to.

I was just trying to help Jan get her belongings. To prove it, I took all her sentimental items (photo books, quilts, etc.) and dropped them off where Jan was living. I photographed everything to prove I had delivered them to her instead of taking them to the dump. I then allowed others to come and take whatever they wanted from the furniture and appliances and then took whatever was left to the dump. What I had to pay in dump fees was no small sum!

On their website, Sound Doctrine posted I had "stolen" $20,000 worth of furnishings.

Also, upon my departure, Tim Williams wrote threatening letters to the leaders of every writer's conference I'd ever taught at saying they would sue if I was invited to be on the faculty in the future. Along with this packet they included their bogus non-compete agreement along with many pages of character assassinations against me.

The claims got more and more outrageous as the attacks kept coming.

Well-known Christian literary agent, Chip MacGregor, even took them on after the WinePress attorney threatened to sue him after Chip made an innocent comment about my story on Facebook saying, "Anyone involved in Christian publishing should read it." Chip went on to post two or three incriminating posts exposing their tactics and calling them to account.

In February 2012, while I was sitting in Dean Smith's Live to Forgive Seminar and trying to forgive what had been done to me, I received a notification about something new posted online with my name. I found a full-blown website at hardtruth.us called "The Hard Truth About Athena Dean." It was a full-on smear job of half-truths, out-of-context quotes, and flat-out lies about me designed to make me look like a nutcase.

One example was a quote from my *Consumed by Success* book where I had talked about the gullibility of Christians making it easy to take advantage of them. The way the quote was posted made it sound like I was boasting about how stupid Christians were and how easy it was to sell them something they didn't need. In context in my book, I was talking about how the Lord had shown me I was taking advantage of people's loyalty and trust by recruiting them into multi-level marketing. I was saying I was wrong and needed to repent. By taking my comment out of context, they made it look evil.

The site also said something like, "The Deans have a habit of attacking the church," making it look as if we were enemies of the Christian church. I was mystified. Who could say that about us? An online search found an old statement made by a leader in the Church of Scientology, saying we were known for attacking the church. Now *that* meant something *totally* different than the quote out of context.

A half-truth publicized on the Hard Truth website was the old indictment for charity fraud from before we became believers. Of course, Tim failed to mention the case against us had been dismissed.

The attacks of Sound Doctrine remind me of the tactics Scientology uses against defectors. Anything and everything is twisted and used to smear reputations and bring credibility into question, even personal information from counseling sessions is used to try to keep them quiet. If this isn't successful, they use every weakness and fault to paint a lurid picture of evil intent to get attention off the abuser and onto the victim. Cults seem to operate the same if you don't conform—with intimidation and manipulation and threats of impending doom.

Right before Thanksgiving in 2012, Tim Williams worked up a twenty-four-page newspaper dedicated to completely smearing and discrediting me and calling me a sociopath and sent it to every residential address within the Enumclaw city limits—all 6,000 of them. They also sent it to every WinePress author, former employee, and freelance editor. They had previously bought up newspaper holders placed next to the *Courier Herald*, *Seattle Times* and *Seattle PI*, so the papers appeared as legitimate journalism. Tim Williams had editors and designers at his disposal, so what he produced looked professional.

By this time, I was in Texas helping my brother with our mom and trying to heal from my nightmare. I am so thankful I didn't know they had pulled this stunt before I made the decision to go to Texas.

I desperately needed the prayers of the many friends who were standing by me. Daily I was amazed at how the Lord was continuing to heal me. It hurt deeply to see those who were once friends believe the lies being disseminated, but God continued to encourage me through those who heard from the Holy Spirit and were seeing through the rhetoric.

One woman who sensed in her spirit something was wrong at WinePress googled my name and saw all the lies and the yellow-journalism junk Sound Doctrine had posted. She encouraged me from Psalm 27:12–14.

> Do not turn me over to the desire of my foes, for false witnesses rise up against me, breathing out violence. I am confident of this: I will see the goodness of the Lord in the land of the living. Wait for the Lord; be strong and take heart and wait for the Lord.

I was determined to be brave and of good courage. I chose to allow my heart to be stout and enduring, to wait for and hope for and *expect* the Lord to expose all needing to be exposed so those who were still in deception could break free.

Ever since the Lord led me out of captivity, out of the hands of the enemy, and placed me back onto the road of truth, He had spoken the words of Psalm 46:10a to me. Over and over and over these words come to my heart: "Be still and know that I am God."

It was sobering to consider the damage I caused with one bad decision. I praise God for His grace that forgives me for the part I played in the WinePress debacle and the lives adversely affected by my actions.

God doesn't promise to free us from the storm, or the circumstance, or the suffering. As we pray, He frees us from our fears about them. As we look to Him for help and cry out to Him in our suffering, He hears us and sets us free.

At first I didn't think I could go to church, after having endured what I had in a "church." But two months after I walked away from the cult, I visited The Summit, an Evangelical Free Church, at the invitation of my friend Jessica Gambill.

There I found a church home where I felt safe. Jessica and her family had attended there after leaving Sound Doctrine about five years before I did. When she began to want out of the cult after seven years, they tried to convince her husband to divorce her, but he didn't fall for it, and the whole family left.

Having recently completed three months of intensive counseling, I was ready for some Christian fellowship. And, wouldn't you know . . . the pastor was just beginning a thirteen-week session on emotionally healthy spirituality. I saw this as the next step of my healing after so many years in a toxic, emotionally-unhealthy church.

For a year, I just sat in my chosen spot in the back on the right side and listened as Pastor Ross Holtz preached each Sunday. The words of grace and God's love were like water to my parched soul. Ross Holtz, from what I observed, loved God, was authentic, humble, sensitive, not afraid to admit his faults, and did not have wandering eyes. He loved his wife and family and he loved his flock. A longing from deep in my heart was voiced as a prayer: *Lord, can I please have a husband like him some day?*

In May of 2012, while all the men were at an annual men's activity called Trout Bums, I attended a get-together of some women in the church. Ross's wife, Cathy, was there, and we enjoyed talking and interacting. About an hour into the evening, she turned to me and said, "You know, Athena, I told Ross if anything ever happens to me, he needs to marry you!"

I smiled on the outside, but I was totally freaked out on the inside. I went home wondering, *Does he know she told me this?* I didn't know what to do with this information, so I distanced myself and just tucked it away inside.

The wonderings about my future were shelved, and my life in the Northwest was uprooted when my brother Jim in San Antonio needed my help after my mom took another fall. She was now ninety and in hospice care at home. My relationship with her hadn't been good for most of my life, and I thought, *I need to go and help.*

NINE

Taking Care of Momma

He heals the brokenhearted and binds up their wounds.

—Psalm 147:3

When I flew down to San Antonio toward the end of November in 2012, my mom's Alzheimer's was so advanced, she still didn't know who I was, the same as she had been on my earlier visit.

As I looked at this frail woman I had always called Mom, it didn't look as if she would be with us long. My brother, influenced by the culture of the South, had begun to call her Momma, so I followed suit.

When I came, I thought my time there would be just a detour, a short assignment, probably over in a few months at the most. But God opened a window of lucidity for Momma the first weekend I was there.

One of my friends from Bible Study Fellowship had a mother with Alzheimer's who had a period of lucidity, enabling my friend to share the gospel with her. They had encouraged me to believe God could do the same with my momma, even though it was hard to imagine when I first saw her.

The first Saturday morning was a quiet one with Jim out on a bike ride and Momma's caregiver, Peggy, off for the weekend. After we had finished breakfast, Momma seemed more aware than normal. I noticed a Thomas Kinkaid gift book filled with pictures and Scriptures in her room and wondered where it came from—she never had inspirational material lying around before. I brought it over to the table and we started looking at the pictures and reading the verses and even singing some of the songs.

When I got to John 3:16, I read out loud and very slowly, "For God so loved the world . . ."

I looked right in my mom's eyes and said, "Momma, do you know how much God loves you?"

"Yes."

I kept reading. "For God so loved the world that He gave His only begotten Son."

"You know that's Jesus, right?"

"Yes."

". . . that whoever believes in Him should not perish but have everlasting life."

"Momma, if you believe in Him, you'll have everlasting life. Do you believe?"

"Yes, I do," my momma said.

"I'm so glad I'm going to see you when I get to heaven, Momma."

"Me too."

Almost right away, the lucidity faded and she went back to her distant look. I noticed Momma seemed more at peace afterwards. She was raised Greek Orthodox, so there would have been residual teaching in her memory bank that God could use to light a spark of faith in her heart.

After the weekend, Momma started making a major turnaround physically and improved dramatically. The short visit I'd anticipated grew to an indefinite open ending as she improved, and I saw how much help Jim needed.

I thought my task would be to help my brother find a small group home to move our Momma into. Then I sensed we should try to keep her at home until the end, if possible. God began to whisper to my heart, *This is your new home.*

Once I knew this was His will, I jumped in with both feet—as I've been known to do—began attending Community Bible Church, joined the choir, got my Texas driver's license, my voter's registration card . . . took the plunge and put down roots—even bought some cowboy boots! Mondays were my day to care for Momma. Jim had Sundays, and the caregiver was with us Tuesdays through Saturdays.

One Monday morning, I moved Momma from her bed to her wheelchair, holding her hands to steady her. I picked up one of her hands and placed her slender fingers in a bowl of water to soak, the first step in giving her a manicure. As I soaked her nails, I thought about what those hands had done. Those wrinkled hands had held me when I was colicky, fed me a concoction of mashed bananas and poi when I couldn't assimilate milk, changed my poopy diapers, and took my hand to help me hold steady as I learned to walk.

Fifty-nine years later, I embraced her as she coughed, held her orange juice and straw for her to drink as she took her meds, changed her diaper on the midnight shift. Sometimes poopy diapers.

Momma still knew what she wanted.

The last time I had applied clear polish. "What color do you want today?"

"Pink."

I thought how hands can hurt or heal . . . exasperate or encourage . . . ignore or ignite.

I pondered always being at odds with her, and how she criticized me for the insatiable desire I had to explore and my nonstop energy.

As I worked on Momma's nails, I remembered how the night before I flew down to Texas to help Jim care for her, I had been blessed with some prayer ministry at my friend Gay Lewis' place called The Hill. During prayer, I completely released any residual unforgiveness I carried towards my momma. I flew to Texas with a new level of forgiveness for her equipped by a new overflowing of the Spirit of God. I wanted to lay my life down for my mom in any way I was needed.

The initial realization that she did the best she knew how to had come right before I visited her for the first time in many years. The prayer session finalized what I believed to be the last vestiges of wounding I received at her hands.

With the healing I had received through prayer, I could use my hands to bless her and meet her needs during her last days, weeks and months on this earth. To love her and bless her and serve her with no regret or sorrow over the past.

Momma's hands had shaped my life, and now mine could be instrumental in blessing her back.

Some days, caring for her didn't seem like a blessing.

It had been a tough week with my momma.

Earlier in the week, I had come into the house to see what was becoming a common sight. Momma was sitting in her wheelchair at the dining room table with her hands covering her face. It was almost like she was begging, *Can't I just go now?*

When I came in from a church conference at four in the afternoon later in the week, she was sitting in the same place with her caregiver beside her. But when she took her hands away from her face, she looked like she'd been punched, as the area around her eyes was black and blue.

"What happened to her eyes?" I asked the caregiver.

"She's been rubbing her eyes and under her eyes almost all day long." All the rubbing had bruised the thin skin underneath her eyes.

Her caregiver and I went into the kitchen where she told me, "I'm concerned. Today's the first day in six years Angela didn't call me by my name." She looked in my eyes and said, "I can see the end is coming soon."

After an amazing service at church that evening, I was having a light-hearted phone conversation with a friend and the topic got around to my mother.

"She's lost so much weight that her dentures don't fit anymore, and she's quit wearing them. Over this week she seems to have almost completely lost her appetite, so her face is looking very gaunt. She's just wasting away to nothing."

As my friend listened sympathetically, I said, "They tell me she's winding down, so it's to be expected."

"This must be really hard on you."

"Oh, I'm doing fine." I pretty much blew it off . . . thinking *I'm doing great.* I thought I was handling everything.

It didn't take long for me to figure out how wrong I was. As I went in to her room to change her diaper that night, it hit me full force. I not only had to change her diaper, but also her wet pajama top. As I took off the old top to help her put on the new one, her body looked like a picture of a Holocaust survivor. She was literally skin and bones. As I helped her get her arms into the sleeves, I held back the tears. When I finished cleaning her up, and pulled a soft blanket up under her chin, I gave her a kiss and told her, "I love you, Momma."

She was silent.

I'd known this was coming for a while, she was in hospice, after all. I just didn't think it would happen quite so fast. I thought we'd still have weeks or months. But the window of time over Christmas had been a gift from the Lord for the three of us to bond and rejoice together. We had taken Momma out for rides to look at the Christmas lights, decorated a tree, put up stockings. We snuggled together watching old Lawrence Welk Christmas programs and even some home movies from the past. I had pointed at myself and said, "Look, Momma, it's me, your wild child, your daughter . . . Athena."

"Really? How can it be you?"

We were moving into a new season.

Before Jim left one Monday morning, he mentioned Momma's toes were hurting her. We talked and decided we should either take her to the podiatrist for a toenail trim, or I could take a whack at it (pun fully intended!).

After feeding Momma breakfast in bed, I decided to take a closer look at her toenails. Not a pretty sight . . . or smell for that matter.

I attempted to trim her toenails but wasn't successful, so to the podiatrist we would have to go. As I cleaned up my failed attempt to minister to her toes, I thought about my reaction to her mangled extremities. At first I was taken aback, but then I felt a surge of compassion for her pain and sought to relieve it by softly washing her disfigurement and wiping away the stench.

Finished, I tucked a blanket around Momma's lap and feet, thinking how tenderly God deals with us. He sees the ugliness of our sin, our attempts to control our lives, which result in our own spiritual disfigurement. He sees our mangled emotions from the pain and losses we have endured, and He is not shocked or taken aback. He pours out His love onto us and wipes away our tears, washes away our stench . . . even on the parts of us we hide from view, those broken places we carefully conceal from those around us for fear of being rejected.

He sees, He loves and He heals—and that's just what He was doing with me.

About half-way through March, Momma was hardly eating at all. The hospice worker told me, "This is part of the dying process. When a person is actively dying, she will refuse food because eating actually causes discomfort and pain." I wasn't prepared to hear what she said next. "I don't think she will make it another ten days." My breath caught, and I felt as if I couldn't get enough air. Emotions I didn't normally feel were swelling up inside me, threatening to overwhelm me.

I knew this was coming, but it always seemed to be far in the future. Reality was setting in.

I took a walk around the block a few times, and the tears kept coming. I looked at the night sky, and even the light of the stars seemed different.

Where were all these feelings coming from? That night I had attended a class on "Respectful Speech" at church where Pastor Louie Kaupp taught on correction and rebuke. At one point during the class, I felt the tears coming when I finally saw what true, loving correction looks like. It was nothing at all like the mean-spirited and harsh rebukes I had experienced.

For those twelve years, shame had been heaped on me. In a Ted Talk called, "Listening to Shame," Brené Brown defines shame as "The intensely painful feeling or experience of believing we are flawed and therefore unworthy of love and belonging." She said shame "absolutely tears apart our sense that we can be and do better." The three components of shame she listed are: "secrecy, silence, and judgment."

I knew this topic intimately as shame was a huge part of the abuse I'd endured. Anytime I was shamed, shunned, publicly humiliated, beat down, or otherwise "disciplined" by the leadership (always with multiple Scriptures to ensure unquestioning obedience), I always ended up believing I was in sin and needed to repent. I believed I had a bitter root, was prideful, or selfish, so my abuse was just the Lord chastening me. Not only did I deserve it, but needed chastening to make it to heaven.

It was considered sinful for me to even *think*, let alone voice the possibility the leadership was abusive or had overreacted in any way. So, when I couldn't place responsibility for the abuse on them, it would naturally be turned back on me.

I had feared for my spiritual life, convinced we were the only *true* church. Walking away from the church to me meant walking away from God. Funny how our statement of faith said we didn't believe we were the only church, but we truly believed we were.

We were taught our leadership was led by the Holy Spirit. They micro-managed every aspect of our lives, large and small. So, I grew strong in the irrational belief they would know "by the Spirit" if I was doubting or struggling or had a bad attitude toward them. This paranoia lead to their version of "walking in the light" and "confession of sin" that was not even my sin and did not need to be confessed.

Shaming and shunning kept me focused on my sin for twelve years. I spent over a decade trying in my own strength to be "good enough" to please the leaders I thought God had placed over me. The truth is, Jesus had already paid the price for my sin. Nothing I could do would make Him love me more, or any less, than He already did.

I think all those things hit me at the same time and exposed some raw spots still needing healing. I was still learning to embrace the pain when it came. Instead of staying "in the moment" and running to God with the pain and allowing Him to comfort me, I usually distracted myself.

Work had always been the drug of choice I used to escape pain. I once felt my tendency was to people please, so I'd take the blame. But I was beginning to see I often moved away, hid in my work, numbed the pain with the distraction of my job, and self-medicated in ways acceptable to others.

In other words, I've used my work to push God—and His work in me—away. When I realized how I'd wasted this opportunity to allow the Lord to comfort me, it made me very sad. But I was grateful God had allowed me to see so clearly how I squandered times of pain.

I knew Momma's passing was imminent. When it finally came, I didn't want the same thing to happen. I wanted to embrace the pain, grieve well, and fully allow the Lord to meet me in the loss.

A few days before Momma passed, I woke up in the middle of the night and saw her light was still on, as was the TV. She had been insisting on leaving them both on when she went to bed the last few days, and my brother must have gone to bed without sneaking in and turning them off.

I tiptoed in and turned off the TV, then the light. I thought something smelled funny but was half asleep so trudged back to bed. As I lay there, I thought, *Maybe she's pooped her diaper again.* Quickly followed, I'm ashamed to say, by *Jim will get it in the morning.* A few minutes ticked by and I couldn't stand it. If she had messed herself, I couldn't just leave it until morning.

I threw back my covers and turned on the hall light outside her room, so she wasn't startled by the direct light.

My worst fears were true. Not only had she messed herself, she'd tried to get the poopy diaper off, so the excrement was everywhere. As I began to pull the sheets back and softly tell her, "I'm going to get you all cleaned up," she pulled at the sheet to try to cover herself and said, "No! Just leave it!"

Compassion overwhelmed me as I used some tough love, gentle but firm, to convince her to cooperate. About forty-five minutes later, she was all cleaned up, new jammies on, new sheets, and was ready to go back to sleep.

I looked into my mom's eyes, traced her face with my fingers and said, "Momma, I love you so much." I patted her softly and said, "Now see how much better it feels to be all clean?"

All the time I was doing my best to thoroughly wipe her down, making sure I had gotten every bit of soil, God was reminding me of how many times I've messed up my life and how He has lovingly cleaned me up each time.

At times, I had tried to protect myself by shooing Him off and saying with my actions, "No! Just leave it . . . I can handle this!" I had found a safe place to hide in my own wounding and the bad choices resulting from those wounds. Stinky and messy had become my new normal.

I'm sure at those moments I "stunk to high heaven," but God didn't turn up His nose, look the other way and just leave me in my mess.

With His grace and mercy, He gently persevered to clean me up because He loves me and doesn't want me to stay in my mess.

God reminded me He is not afraid of our sinful messes . . . and not afraid to turn the light on to penetrate our darkness, so He can clean us up and make us new.

Momma died on April 5, 2013. Her bittersweet memorial service was held on July 13, 2013 when the family could get together. It was a major landmark for me, and an amazing restoration as I had the opportunity to publicly honor my momma, after a lifetime of not doing so. After thirteen or fourteen years of alienation, the family came together. I renewed long-lost relationships with cousins, aunts, and uncles, and saw my younger brother, a professional musician who goes by Arthur Lee Land, in person for the first time in many years. Best of all, I could voice my deep sorrow for the way I hurt my family members by refusing to go to my father's bedside when he was dying.

Momma's nemesis, I was head-strong, boisterous, adventurous, and talkative. Try as she might, she just could not contain me; mothering me was a serious challenge.

Everything had to be just so with my mom. I rebelled against those expectations, never trying to meet them, no wonder we were never close! I never felt as if I could ever measure up, and she felt like I wasn't trying hard enough.

Right before I came down to Texas to visit in January, 2012, I watched the movie *Divine Secrets of the Ya-Ya Sisterhood*. I watched a realization unfold in one of the characters about a time in her life when her mother was having a nervous breakdown, but she felt her mom was mean to her and abusive. Her epiphany came when she realized her mom had been going through an emotionally devastating time in her life.

God used that movie to help me see all her negative nagging and pushing me to do better were not attempts to hurt me. She was doing the best she knew how with a precocious and high-maintenance daughter who was born driven.

My father used to say about me, "Athena wants . . . and she wants *hard!*"

I cannot imagine what it was like for her to have a daughter like me!

The last four months with my mom before she died was a wonderful time of bonding with her. God taught me so many things through simply caring for her. I was so grateful He had opened that window of lucidity so I could share the gospel with her on my first weekend there. So many simple things reminded me of God's unending grace, His everlasting mercy, and His unconditional love: painting her nails, changing her diapers, brushing her hair, and spoon-feeding her.

I was not the same person as when I arrived in San Antonio on November 29. My heart and the depth of compassion I was learning to feel for others had grown in ways I couldn't even express. As painful as many moments were over this time, I wouldn't trade them for anything.

I made my peace with Momma and with my older brother, Jim. Momma made peace with God, so I know I'll see her again one of these days.

When I asked God to restore my life after the devastation I endured in the cult, I had no idea caring for my momma would be one of the ways He would bring restoration and how much it would mean to me.

What a good God He is! I can only rejoice in the privilege I've had to finally become the daughter my momma always wanted me to be.

TEN

Speed Bumps and Benches

Be still, and know that I am God; I will be exalted among the nations,
I will be exalted in the earth.

—Psalm 46:10

My time in Texas seemed to be all about learning how to wait, how to be still, and how to fight against the parts in me still seeking the spotlight and wanting to make things happen. "Be still and know" was the Scripture I had taken for the year even before I left Enumclaw to go help take care of my momma. Being still was the hard part for me, a repenting type-A doer. It was one of the most difficult things I've ever had to do, yet one of the most rewarding of all.

As I had settled in to my life in Texas, I thought, *Maybe this will be my new forever home. Maybe God will bring Mr. Right into my life here.* I loved San Antonio and had great anticipation as to how the Lord would work all things together for good.

While I was still coaching writers on getting published on a small scale, daily I wondered what I was going to do with the rest of my life. I was committed to helping out with Momma for as long as I was needed, but I was still restless.

Two weeks after my Mom went to heaven, a totally unexpected door opened. So many times over the previous four months I had struggled with not knowing what would be next for me. I had pouted, whined, and wept. But God would always whisper, *Be still. Just be present in the moments I give you with your momma. Don't worry about tomorrow.* I had to let my dreams go and just stay focused on the task at hand.

One Thursday, I almost didn't make it to my new friend Anna Quesada's Christian Women's Small Business Expo on April 18.

"I've saved you a table," she told me, urging me to come. After thinking I could potentially make some contacts for my coaching services, at the last minute, I changed my mind. In a large room in the Comfort Inn, I set up my table and was ready for some divine appointments.

Just before the speaker's session began, Karen Ann, the rep from KSLR, the local Christian talk-radio station, came by my table and we chatted for a bit. Toward the end of our chat, I asked, "Does KSLR have any shows that interview authors?" I was always thinking about my authors who might need to get some exposure.

Her response floored me. "How'd *you* like to have a radio show?"

"Uh . . . wow! Let me pray about it and get back to you!" She gave me her card, and I committed to follow up with her.

The meeting was beginning, and I couldn't get away to pray, but right then a memory flashed across my mind. A few weeks after arriving in San Antonio, I had attended a training class at the Christ Healing Center. As we prayed in small groups for one another, a ministry staffer prayed for me (not knowing anything about my media background) and said she "saw" a picture of me sitting behind a microphone with a headset on, as well as a gold microphone in a black velvet box.

After we had finished praying, she said, "I sense the Lord is saying you are going to do something in radio. It's going to be a platform where you will speak for Him."

After the session, my mind had made a list everyone I knew in the radio business. Wheels were turning about a strategy to get a radio show going. With my background in both being interviewed extensively and interviewing others over the last twenty-five years, the idea of doing something in talk radio totally excited me.

As I mulled these things over in my heart, I began to wonder, *Is God going to have me do something new?*

As if in answer to those thoughts, a few weeks later, at another meeting, a woman who didn't know anything about me told me, "I feel the Lord wants you to know He is going to have you do something totally new."

It took everything in me to resist the urge to reconnect with all my radio friends I'd made over the years of my career in publishing. But I was determined to wait. *If this is God, He will bring it to pass.*

I saw these incidents not as coincidental, but as God confirming He was in this. I made an appointment to meet with the management at the radio station. By the end of the conversation, Baron Wiley, the general manager of sales, suggested I do a one-hour interview show for women in a Saturday morning slot. I was dumbfounded. Everything I had always wanted to do—speak to women about God's goodness on the radio and from a platform, using my gifts and talents for Him—was literally falling into my lap.

This was a huge step of faith. Despite my excitement, moving into a full-time radio ministry was a scary transition requiring a huge amount of trust for me. God met me in this adventure and provided the funding needed in a completely miraculous way. He proved Himself faithful over and over in amazing ways in this new venture.

But the opportunity did not come without an all-out assault from the evil one. I was just sure the station management would see the online smear campaign the cult had instigated against me. My mind nervously went to the worst outcome. *They won't want to take a risk on me because of all the Sound Doctrine garbage online.*

I wanted with everything in me to call the station and do preemptive damage control, but felt God was saying, *Just let me fight this battle for you.* I surrendered again and allowed Him to take charge.

It wasn't long before a follow-up appointment was set for me to go in.

After making a demo tape I waited for the final green light from Salem corporate before signing the contract. Always Faithful Radio went live on Saturday, June 1, 2013 from 11 a.m. to noon, central time, on AM 630 KSLR, and streaming live. The hour's format was interviews with two or three individuals per show, many who were my author friends or speakers from across the country.

With the birth of Always Faithful Radio, God had given me an amazing open door to walk through—allowing me to have a huge influence for good on women in this region.

After each program, I held a "Continue the Conversation" no-host lunch at El Jarro's Mexican restaurant. One Saturday when I arrived at

El Jarro's after the program, a woman named Babbie hobbled in late on crutches with a portable oxygen tank. She'd caught the last thirty minutes of the program and felt the Lord was telling her to come and join us for lunch. She turned her car around twice on the way but persevered in obeying what she felt the Lord was telling her.

Sitting across from me, she began sharing health issues ranging from extreme pain all over her body, near deafness in one ear, poor eyesight, general stiffness and mobility issues, bunions, hammertoes, knee pain, shoulder and neck pain. Then Babbie said, "My pastor never teaches on healing. I'm struggling with that; I really need healing."

Lizzie Smiley, my in-studio guest leaned over and said, "My friend Hillary Akromis is on her way to lunch . . . and she operates in the gift of healing."

This should be interesting, I thought.

When Hillary arrived, the only seat open was next to Babbie. I watched in awe at this divine appointment. Not only had Hilary been raised in the same denomination as Babbie, but, as an accomplished athlete, she understood her pain, having spent four years with excruciating knee pain, two years on crutches, and with severe back pain for fifteen years afterwards. God had healed her miraculously some years ago, and she often prayed for others to be healed.

After I left the restaurant at 2, Hillary prayed for Babbie and all the pain in her body left, and she walked around the restaurant without her crutches. God had used the Always Faithful radio program to orchestrate a divine appointment!

The opportunity to have this hour-long program to encourage and bless women was a great lesson to me of the power of prayer and waiting on God to bring it to pass. He is faithful! As I stepped out to go into full-time radio ministry, I came under the covering of Commissioned to Every Nation (www.cten.org). This proved to be God's leading for a season in my life, and it was confirmed in so many ways, financially and otherwise.

When I think about how lovingly, how gently God has led me . . . whispering to me to just trust Him, be still, and let Him fight my battles, I weep with thankfulness. As hard as it was to do, I kept surrendering, I kept allowing Him to have His way. I am *so* glad I did. It would have been so easy for me to just be Athena . . . the Athena who makes things happen in her own abilities and strength. But how glad I am I stepped back and allowed God to be in charge . . . His plan is always better than mine!

ELEVEN

Single and Surrendered

. . . be transformed by the renewing of your mind. Then you will be able to test and approve what God's will is—his good, pleasing and perfect will.

—Romans 12:1–2

It was August and hot in an especially Texas kind of way.

A friendship with a man I had hoped would develop hadn't progressed. I wasn't getting the sponsors I needed to fund my new Always Faithful radio show. My type-A personality wanted to do something about both issues, but I didn't know what to do. An anxious feeling in the pit of my stomach reminded me of what I didn't want to think about. *Maybe this isn't going to work out.*

With my thoughts and emotions all over the map, I talked with close friends Jay and Karen Peavler.

"Woah, slow down, Athena! You've got to give God time to work," Jay said.

"I know. I know. But I can't stop thinking about ways to fix this."

"That's the time to 'take every thought captive,'" Karen said, referring to 2 Corinthians 10:5. "Replace those thoughts with truth from God's Word."

I knew they were right. I had to get my mind centered on God and His Word. But I was lonely.

Whining and complaining, I let God know in no uncertain terms I was ready for a husband! I had no interest in dating unless it was someone I would be interested in marrying. So, I waited and I waited. No dates. No nothing but my intermittent whining to God. It felt as if every door had slammed in my face.

I must be ready now for my Prince Charming! After all, I had experienced so much healing and growth after my twelve years of deception. I was sure I was ready, but nothing seemed to be happening.

The good choice I made to avoid men while in recovery and the encouragement from the Lord to be still, kept me on an even keel much of the time. But, over and over again, I came to a place of impatience in my heart. About eight months into my healing journey, I felt I was making major headway and determined I must be ready. Notice *I* determined . . . it certainly wasn't something coming out of my time with the Lord!

"Athena, you don't need to wait for God to bring you your man," a friend advised. "My goodness, you're a grown woman and can make grown up decisions about who to date! Quit trying to spiritualize everything . . . there is nothing sinful about meeting someone on the Internet!"

When I first came down to Texas, I was invited to a singles group at one of the large churches in the area but didn't meet anyone I was interested in. My next resort was an online dating site for Christians.

I even got sucked into a few Facebook messages from men I didn't know who sounded as if they were authentic and looking for a serious relationship. I admit it, I was vulnerable and still easily persuaded by words of affirmation.

Even then, I just couldn't bring myself to try to make it happen using the online dating service. I'd sign back in and try it for a while, and then be convicted to stop. A few weeks later, I'd feel lonely again and boom—I was back at it again. But God just shut me down every time. I'm certainly not saying it isn't the right vehicle for some women. God can use anything to bring people together. I just knew it wasn't right for me. It felt too much as if I was orchestrating things rather than allowing Him to do it.

Before I moved down to Texas, I found someone on Facebook who had been a widower for fifteen years. He looked like "my type" and it appeared as if he was a strong Christian. Because I liked what I saw, I went on to convince myself God had orchestrated this. I spent the next six months thinking he was the one God had been saving me for. In my journal during this time, it was as if I was trying to convince God this was a good match. But down deep, I could tell I was trying to sell God on what I wanted . . . on what my eyes could see . . . on what looked good to me.

While in my heart I longed to have a godly husband, I didn't trust myself to make a good choice anymore. My willingness to wait and stay single for as long as I did wasn't exactly based on my saintly spiritual depth. Nope. Far from it. I was protecting myself, scared to death I'd be duped once again and make another bad choice. After all, I had made some pretty bad choices in men, both as mates and leaders to follow.

I continued my wrestling match with God in my journal, writing, "Lord, where is the man you've been saving for me?"

After my counseling ended, I attended the Florida Christian Writers' Conference to teach a few classes, thrilled to once again be included among my publishing peers. Afterwards, I spent some down time alone in a rustic little bungalow on the beach at Anna Maria Island.

While I so enjoyed my time with the Lord there, I was conflicted and lonely. Everywhere I looked an image sent me reeling. Couples walked the beach hand in hand. Tables for two were filled with couples enjoying each other's company. Walking through the marina early one morning, I passed a boat with twin bikes leaning up against the railing of the deck. Even this simple picture of togetherness dissipated my happy mood, turning it to discontent in a split second. My emotions plummeted into the depths of despair. *Will I ever find a godly man to spend the rest of my days with?*

Just four months later, I reconnected with a former pastor/writer friend I'd met many years before. He had gone through a horrific divorce a year and a half earlier, and had lived through many traumas in his life. After spending a few hours in a Starbucks sharing our stories, I felt a real bonding had occurred. He was younger than me, not exactly my type, and nowhere near ready for a relationship, but I convinced myself God must have orchestrated our reconnection with marriage in mind. I was over-spiritualizing again!

I thought about all the ways he matched the items on my "list." Not a flirt, he loved God, and had a heart for wounded people. He didn't match my entire list, but I saw the circumstance of us meeting again after so many years as God's doing. I would just have to settle for a partial fulfillment of the list. I was determined to wait for as long I had to until he was ready for a new relationship. In the meantime, we were good friends, but that was all.

My good friend had a ministry of helping adult men who were survivors of childhood sexual abuse. He also taught Christians how to grieve well after the loss of a loved one. I was smitten by the opportunity to be part of a ministry helping so many broken people. But no matter how much I tried to convince myself that this was God's will for me, eventually it became obvious I was sincere, but sincerely wrong.

I wanted him to be Mr. Right, even though he wasn't even my type, was eight years younger than me, and still traumatized from a bitter divorce.

This relationship would have been me settling for less than God's best. But I had made a case for the potential relationship in my head and heart and sold myself on it, even when I continued to have little niggling doubts about my decision to wait for this man.

What I was exhibiting is called confirmation bias. Sometimes it's called "my side bias." We all do it! We have a belief, then we look for information confirming our belief and ignore information contradicting that belief. I did the same thing with the cult, always looking for anything confirming it was right so I wouldn't have to admit I was wrong!

My flesh wanted this relationship to be *the one*. I had convinced myself his ministry was something worthwhile to which I could dedicate the rest of my life. *I will just have to wait for him.*

A few months after I had decided this, I was given a gift during a general session of the Chosen to Grow Women's Conference. Each woman there received the same bright green flower pot with various words gracing the base. Wouldn't you know it . . . the word on mine said, *Patience*.

Yes, Lord, I know I have to be patient, thinking the Lord was telling me to keep on waiting for this man. I had obviously jumped to conclusions, when the Lord was just encouraging me to be patient in general.

In my daily devotions I wasn't sensing any direction from God. He would just whisper, *Be still and know that I am God.* The morning of August 16, I read the day's selection in *Streams in the Desert.*[2] Truth resonated in my heart:

> Must life be a failure for one compelled to stand still in enforced inaction and see the great throbbing tides of life go by? No; victory is then to be gotten by standing still, by quiet waiting. It is a thousand times harder to do this than it was in the active days to rush on in the columns of stirring life. It requires a grander heroism to stand and wait and not lose heart and not lose hope, to submit to the will of God, to give up work and honors to others, to be quiet, confident and rejoicing, while the happy, busy multitude go on and away. It is the grandest life "having done all, to stand."
>
> —J. R. Miller

While the truth of this resonated in my heart, I balked. *Stand still? Quiet waiting? I'm tired of waiting. Haven't I waited long enough?*

The encouragements from God to "be still," the creative confirmation in a gift to remind me to be patient . . . all whispered the same thing to me . . . the right one will be worth the wait. But I was hearing what I wanted to hear, not what He was saying!

---

[2] L. B. E. Cowman, *Streams in the Desert* (Grand Rapids: Zondervan, 1996).

Then God began to send me illustrated examples of what He wanted me to do.

One day walking home from Starbucks where I had gone for a little break from my routine, I watched as a little white car came flying down the road in my neighborhood, ignoring the two sets of speedbumps right ahead. Ignoring the directive of the "Speed Bumps Ahead" sign, the vehicle didn't slow down in the slightest as it hit the bumps, and even caught a little air. It must have given the driver a good jolt.

That's me. I was a "get-it-done-fast" kind of person. Was this a little hint from God to get me to slow down? Was I just ignoring His speed bumps and racing forward?

Oh, Lord . . . that is so me! Forgive me for not being sensitive to your speed bumps in my life!

God was so good to provide the speed-bump visual. He was intentionally reminding me to slow down!

Then there were all the benches I kept noticing when I walked around the neighborhood. Wooden benches under trees, an iron bench beside the still waters of a lake, benches here, benches there, benches everywhere. I began stopping at the benches I saw, sitting for a bit, and tuning my heart in to God. "Be still and know" came frequently to mind, as well as other Scriptures about resting, taking a break, and just being still with God. I meditated on, "My sheep listen to my voice; I know them, and they follow me" (John 10:27). Then I began taking pictures of all my resting places so I wouldn't forget.

God was obviously up to something in my life. I knew He wanted me to slow down. He was at work in the waiting, even when I didn't sense it or enjoy it. He wanted me to pause . . . to wait . . . to surrender . . . to learn to trust Him and His ways . . . to keep my eyes focused on Him rather than on what I longed for.

One day while walking in our neighborhood of older homes lined with shade trees, I again sensed God speaking to my heart.

How fast do those trees grow?

The answer came to my heart—*slowly.*

Benches offer breaks and rest.

Speed bumps are warnings.

If I raced from one event to the next, propelled by my own agenda, I would miss what God was doing around me and in me. And I'd miss hearing His voice.

The visual cues of my surroundings were showing me the correlation between slowing down, spending more time with Him, learning to wait, growing in faith, and *trusting* God. His voice comes in a whisper. "After the earthquake came a fire, but the Lord was not in the fire. And after the fire came a gentle whisper" (1 Kings 19:12). I needed to listen for that still, small voice, the gentle whisper, and allow Him to do His work in my heart.

So, I guess my first good choice was to commit myself to getting healthy, spiritually, emotionally, mentally, relationally. Until I had myself on level ground, growing in spiritual and emotional maturity, I had no business even thinking about dating or marriage. I must admit, this good choice was bathed and undergirded by the Lord who gently and persistently reminded me to "be still and know that He is God."

TWELVE

The Elephant in the Room

Love is blind and lovers cannot see
The pretty follies that themselves commit.

—Shakespeare, *The Merchant of Venice*

I was in Texas for good, as far as I was concerned, and wouldn't be returning to Washington.

One day I heard from a friend the tragic news that Pastor Ross Holtz's wife, Cathy, had passed away on September 30, 2013. After her diagnosis, she had only lived for 126 days. She ran into the arms of Jesus just twenty-five days after it was determined the chemo wasn't working. I was shocked as I had only heard about her cancer a few days before she passed.

I wasn't sure why Ross's Facebook posts never came up on my feed, but I was out of the loop on everything. We hadn't been in touch since I said goodbye to my church family at The Summit and left for Texas.

But I had never forgotten asking God to give me a man *like* Ross Holtz. I was so drawn to his humility, his love for his wife and family, his lack of flirtatiousness, and deep love for God.

Then I remembered how Cathy had said he should marry me if anything happened to her.

About three weeks later, I received a LinkedIn acceptance of my request to connect with Ross. It was something I'd sent about eighteen months earlier, and he just finally had gotten around to logging in to LinkedIn after cancer took his wife.

This sent me into a full-on tizzy. Since Cathy had encouraged him to marry me if anything ever happened to her, I wondered, *Is Ross showing interest in me?* Obstinately, I reasoned, *This has to be the work of the enemy trying to distract me from what God is calling me to do—wait for my friend.*

God was at work in my life, but I didn't understand what He was doing. It didn't line up with what I perceived was His will. Was I rebuking God by thinking I was doing battle with the enemy? In the middle of my tizzy, I fell to my knees and let my Bible open to where it may—not a recommended way to receive guidance. When these verses in Romans jumped out at me, I was convinced God was speaking to me through it.

> Therefore, I urge you, brothers and sisters, in view of God's mercy, to offer your bodies as a living sacrifice, holy and pleasing to God — this is your true and proper worship. Do not conform to the pattern of this world, but be transformed by the renewing of your mind. Then you will be able to test and approve what God's will is — his good, pleasing and perfect will. (Rom. 12:1–2)

Since I thought waiting for my friend was God's will for me, I saw my waiting as a sacrifice of sorts, especially since I had to keep convincing myself he was the one.

What if Ross is thinking about a relationship with me? I'd better set the issue straight about him and me. I'll just e-mail him and address the "elephant in the room."

If I had thought about it twice, I would have known there was no "elephant in the room!" Obviously, he wouldn't be having ideas about another relationship three weeks after his beloved wife of forty-nine years had slipped into eternity!

But I couldn't get it off my mind. So, on October 18, 2013, I e-mailed Ross to let him know, in no uncertain terms, God was saving me for someone else, just in case he had any ideas. It sounds laughable now, but I thought I was obeying God. Funny how He sometimes uses our naïve ways to accomplish what He wants to in our lives!

I pressed "send" on my e-mail to Ross, telling him God had made it clear I was to wait for someone else. But I was not yet admitting to myself my friend was showing no signs of being ready for a deeper relationship with me.

Then I wrote this on Facebook, "Ever felt like God was asking you to take a step of faith, and so you drew a line in the sand, or burned some bridges, out of obedience . . . and then wondered if you were crazy? That's kinda how I'm feeling right about now . . . crazy good, but still a little crazy."

Much later Ross told me the e-mail I sent had caught him off guard, shocked and surprised him. "I didn't realize there was any elephant in the room," he said. Then he moved on to feeling he had been dumped when we weren't even going together! When he thought about it, he felt flattered I would even approach him. He wondered who would want to marry a sixty-seven-year-old pastor who wasn't wealthy and had grown kids living in his home.

Ross thought long and hard about how to respond. He didn't want to hurt my feelings or say anything offensive. After a few days, I received back a gracious response. Among other things, he said, "I don't find the thought of being married to you unpleasant, but I didn't take Cathy's words as prophetic." But he added, "I want to make sure we stay friends in the future." Later, he told me he thought I was interesting and attractive. But it had been just weeks since his wife Cathy had died, so, of course, he hadn't seriously considered the idea of remarrying.

Part of what was at work when I sent the message was the baggage I still carried from the twelve years of legalistic false doctrine I'd been deceived with. We were taught to think the only way something could be God's will was if we didn't want to do it. If I had to sacrifice and surrender a desire of my heart, then it must be God's will. I'd eventually find joy in doing His will. If it was something I wanted to do, it must be of the devil.

I read into Romans 12:1–2 the belief that waiting for someone I wasn't truly in love with was my way of offering myself as a living sacrifice. While Ross was way more my type and more of the kind of man I could see myself marrying, he must only be God's pleasing will . . . not His perfect will. I would just have to give up what would make me the happiest to do God's perfect will.

I had come to a completely wrong conclusion based on erroneous thinking and my confirmation bias! So, to offer my body as a living sacrifice, I drew a line in the sand when I wrote the e-mail to Ross. I felt I had to let him know I wasn't available, even though Cathy had suggested he marry me, as God had made it "clear" to me I was to wait for my friend.

I felt sorry for myself and was jealous of other women who were happily married. It was taking way too long to wait for the guy I thought God wanted me to wait for. I began to wonder, *have I missed God altogether?* Would He ever bring me a godly husband?

I finally resigned myself to being single for the rest of my life and was determined to be content.

God continued to whisper, *Be still,* in my ear, but I never fully received and obeyed that word in this area of my life. I was tired of waiting! I wanted a husband like other women had, one who would love me as Christ loved the church, lay down his life for me, and protect me.

Knowing what I know now, having Him provide over and above anything I could have ever asked for in a husband, brings me to tears. I now realize how little I trusted Him and how impatient I was. I'm sure I missed many lessons He was trying to teach me because I was just so wrapped up in myself and because of what I felt I was "owed" after I had lost so much.

But, praise God, He overlooked all of that when I finally repented for my lack of obedience. When I finally surrendered to His will and let go of mine, everything changed. This time I wasn't repenting in hopes He would finally give me what I wanted. I didn't give to get. I didn't check the box to feel better as I'd done so often in the past.

And what a faithful God He is to forgive, to restore, to redeem . . . even after all my emotional rants inside my head . . . even after my struggle to trust Him with my life. He has some broad shoulders to be able to take what I dished out and love me anyway.

At choir practice for our first service of the new year—2014—worship pastor Ray Jones shared the plan for the service at Community Bible Church.

"The altar time mid-worship is going to be a bit different. I'm going to ask the congregation to make some New Year's resolutions."

I smiled at my neighbor, wondering where the director was going with this.

"These are the most important resolutions you could possibly make."

My interest piqued.

"I'm going to ask you to first listen to God. And second, to obey whatever He tells you to do."

I hear you Lord! Loud and clear.

Then he announced the three songs we'd be working on for the Saturday night and Sunday morning services. First there was "Awake My Soul." I had already chosen the song as my theme for the new year. Then there was "Speak to Me," and "I Surrender."

The message was coming through—finally!

Sunday, right before the 11 a.m. service, Marlene Salcher, an author who I had coached through the publishing of her book, proudly handed me a copy of her first book. I looked down at the attractive cover and the words of the title jumped out at me: *God Speaks to Me? Tuning in to the Living God.*

God was putting an exclamation point on what He had been showing me. I would have to trust Him. When He finally did bring redemption, restoration and the relationship I so strongly desired, I could look back and see the refinement He worked in the waiting.

THIRTEEN

Into Loving Arms

Arise my darling, my beautiful one, and come with me.
See! The winter is past; the rains are over and gone.
Flowers appear on the earth;
The season of singing has come.

—Song of Songs 2:10–12

By the end of 2013, God was helping me to see how much I had tried to make the relationship I was waiting for happen. As He worked in my heart, I spent my entire New Years' Eve repenting for my idolatry, for pursuing, for assuming I knew what God was doing.

If this is not the man You have for me, then I surrender my will, and what I thought my future was going to be like. Have Your way, Lord.

On January 8, 2014, I landed in the emergency room in intense pain and then into surgery to have my gallbladder removed. While still in the hospital, I received a text from a friend saying WinePress was closing its doors.

Two days later the question was posed to me . . . would I be willing to return to Washington to start a company to help the orphaned WinePress authors?

I'd been telling God for fourteen months I was *not* returning to Washington. There were too many reminders of the trauma and the loss and the abuse I'd endured. So, when the question came, I was a little taken aback. But I committed to pray and ask for godly counsel from my family and friends I knew I could trust. All responses were positive.

On January 14, not even a week after my surgery, I felt confident this was God's will. I had been wrong about God's will about the man whom I thought I had to wait for. But this time there was a centered knowing, a peace, about going back to Washington.

I had already purchased roundtrip tickets to come to CA and WA to visit my grandkids. Then the thought came to me: *You won't be using your return ticket.*

As I prayed through the transition back to Washington I felt compelled to try to stay under my Commission to Every Nation (CTEN) covering. If I was going back into publishing, I would expand my mission statement to include publishing along with radio ministry. To do so, I had to explain my plans to CTEN and my pastoral care couple and see if they would approve it. They asked to whom I would be accountable, where I would worship, and who would be my pastor.

Of course I wanted to go back to The Summit—it was my church. My pastoral care couple called Ross and asked him many questions. Could he meet with me weekly? Would he be my overseer? Ross was happy to oblige.

About that time, I began to wonder what God was up to.

As my time to travel back to Washington drew closer, Ross and I increased our communication by messaging on Facebook. Just before I left San Antonio on the 23rd of January, Ross told me, "I'm glad you are coming back to Washington." He added, "Call me some evening . . . I have a lot of free time on my hands these days."

My heart started pounding. This man was pursuing me! This was one of the things high on my list of what I wanted in a man. I felt the man God had for me would pursue me, not the other way around.

After my New Year's surrender to the will of God, I never would have guessed I would be going back to Washington just a few weeks later, back into publishing and back to The Summit and to Ross!

Sitting in the Sacramento airport, waiting for my shuttle to Redding to go see my son, I finally got up the nerve to call Ross as he had suggested.

What a phone call! Within the first five minutes Ross asked to take me out on what would be my first date in fourteen years! A sense rose in my heart that Ross was the man God had chosen for me. All the feelings of respect and admiration came flooding back I'd had when sitting in his congregation asking God if I could have a man like him someday. We both started asking questions to see if the other fit the requirements we each had on our "list." It didn't take long to find out each non-negotiable on our lists was checked off and confirmed. It was quickly proving to be a perfect match.

Ross picked me up at SeaTac airport when I arrived in Washington on January 27. Walking off the concourse and into his welcoming hug felt like coming home. We talked for hours, and I was stunned at what I learned.

Once Cathy knew her cancer was terminal, she told Ross he should remarry and quickly, if he wanted to. She told him her list of potential wives, and my name was still at the top of the list.

He also said if God hadn't taken me to Texas, and I had still been a member of The Summit, he wouldn't have felt free to date me. As an unwritten policy in the church, pastors didn't date in the congregation because of the tension it causes between people. God took me away and brought me back right at the right time . . . amazing!

Just three months before, September 5, my daughter had written me an e-mail saying, "God is releasing the word *marriage* to you and is sending you your match made in heaven." I thought this was referring to my friend I was waiting for. But, it was all about Ross and me, and I couldn't see it at the time. Turns out the word from the Lord through Roby was right.

While God was bringing me to a place of realizing I'd been trying to make this other relationship happen, Ross was asking God to send him a wife. He wanted someone to spend time with and didn't want to spend the summer alone. He even began telling his staff he was going to get married—he just didn't know to whom yet!

Two days after I had arrived home in Washington, I knew I was in love with Ross. During the two weeks before returning, I wondered if God was orchestrating something for the two of us. I knew I was not to initiate. When Ross brought up the subject of marriage in his natural and unpretentious way, I knew with certainty, *This is it!* It was almost instantaneous! He said he knew it when I walked off the plane and into his arms.

We both knew what we had been looking for and dreaming of in a relationship. As we talked further, every single line item on our individual lists of what we wanted in a mate got a resounding "check."

I had quite a list! I wanted someone who was spiritually mature, well respected, ministry minded, willing to deal with his own issues, humble, and musical. He couldn't be a flirt—and not a porn addict! I longed for someone who would initiate the relationship so I would know it was meant to be and not just me rushing ahead. Being financially stable was important. I hoped for someone who was strong but not controlling or legalistic.

Ross's list for a wife included a strong believer but not a syrupy-sweet, typical piano-playing pastor's wife type (my apologies to those pastors' wives who play the piano!). He hoped for a classy, confident, attractive woman who was a good conversationalist. He threw in playful, and would you believe it, strong-willed! Even one who would enjoy a glass of wine with him.

Ross is laid back and secure enough in his manhood not to be intimidated or threatened by my strength or giftings—a wonderful bonus for me. In considering asking me to be his wife, Ross made sure there was no possibility of a reconciliation with Chuck who had been married twice after our divorce and was happily married at the time, and still is.

God truly was indeed blessing me for being willing to wait for the right guy and Ross for being faithful and true for forty-nine years of marriage.

As I got to know him better, just as I had suspected, I found he is a wonderful, stable family man, as evidenced by his children and grandchildren who love him fiercely. What you see is what you get—at church and home.

Ross Holtz was born in Los Gatos, Calif. to Hank and Bernice Holtz. Mostly Norwegian and some German from his father's side, he is a full-blood Scott on his mother's side. He had accepted Christ at the age of six and felt called by God to preach at the age of eight. While he was always aware of God working in his life, during his teen years and beyond, he ran from the Lord's will for his life. With his band, The Village Criers, he played twelve-string guitar and was a vocalist. The band experienced a short stint of fame after cutting two singles, one with Delta Records, and played at the Monterey Folk Festival, opening for Mahalia Jackson to an audience of 10,000.

After his one-and-only girlfriend, Cathy, became pregnant at seventeen, they married and he went to work to support his new family. At first he worked as a checker and stocker in Safeway's management training program, then branched out in sales in the food industry.

After a personal revival at age twenty-six, he was encouraged to go to seminary and offered a scholarship at the Criswell Center for Biblical Studies in Dallas. With his newly minted credentials with the Southern Baptist denomination, Ross took his first pastorate in Carbonado, Wash., about twenty miles from Enumclaw. He began working on his master's degree online and grew the church from fifty to 250 in five years' time in a town of 560 people.

Members of his congregation at The Summit, the Evangelical Free church he founded in 1987, say they love his humility, his love for family, his wisdom in handling conflict and difficult situations. He is respected as one who has integrity and a long track record of faithful service. He completed his master's at Columbia Evangelical Seminary and was awarded an honorary doctorate in 2016.

Ross has been in the ministry for forty years. Once he was asked to put in his resumé as a potential successor to Chuck Swindoll but turned down the opportunity to candidate for the position.

The most comfortable place for Ross is in the pulpit preaching and he is very good at it. I've heard him referred to as "the best preacher on the Plateau." He does not compromise the Word of God to make people feel good, so he has certainly not always been liked by those who would prefer their ears "tickled." But he is a lover not a hater. He would rather have The Summit known for what we are *for* rather than what we are *against*. Just about the polar opposite of Sound Doctrine!

He believes in churches working together and partners with three or four other local churches on the Plateau for various ministry opportunities. He is a "father" to younger pastors and has been a true cheerleader of men's ministries. The Summit's men's ministry is one of the most successful in our EFC region and the most effective in drawing men together towards living a life dedicated to Christ. In recognition, in 2014 he was named "Pastor of the Year" for the National Coalition of Ministries to Men.

He just loves living where he does. He has lived in this small town and house for thirty years. Often, when we walk into a restaurant or business in town, he is greeted by all sorts of people. Every so often he will turn to me with a twinkle in his eyes and ask, "Did I ever tell you I love small towns?"

His children love him dearly, and he is clearly the patriarch of the Holtz Clan. They see him as one who has been a strong and wonderful example of a father who loves unconditionally and extends grace. He often says, "I would rather stand before God and be guilty of extending too much grace and being too generous." His family motto is Infractus Quod Invictus ("Broken but Undefeated"). His father told him, "You cannot defeat a man who will not be defeated." So when his prodigal son came home years ago after wandering off into drugs, Ross acted like the father of the prodigal son in the Bible. He created a family crest with Infractus Quod Invictus on it, had it embroidered onto black jackets for his children, and welcomed his son home with the jacket and a clan ring.

We didn't announce our intention to marry to the church family until Ross had time to talk with his adult children and the two oldest grandsons. He wasn't looking for permission, just agreement. The kids and grandkids had suffered a huge loss. Their loss was now enabling me to experience great gain. Ross didn't rush them but encouraged them as they processed their grief.

Ross is so committed to his family that he made sure they all knew about our plans to marry before we committed to a date and announced it to the church. After the betrayal I had previously experienced at the hands of the men in my life, his loyalty was all important.

With the Holtz family all supportive of their dad's decision, we made the big announcement to the church family on the weekend of March 15 and 16, 2014. Our wedding date was set for June 13, but technically, we had been engaged since the beginning of February.

I was so moved by the analogy God gave Ross to share on the day of our announcement. He recalled to the congregation the time when

Cathy found out she was pregnant with their second child. She was overly emotional as she could not see how she could possibly love another child as much as she loved her firstborn, Bret. But, as time went on, she not only loved Thad well, but Nathan, and Elizabeth too. She found she had the capacity to love each child as an individual without taking away any of the love for the others. He told the congregation his love for me in no way diminished the love he had for Cathy during their forty-nine years of marriage.

Isn't God's faithfulness amazing? A good friend recently told me she'd been sharing my love story with some ladies. She had told them how evident God's blessing is in my life for my being willing to repent and obey His call. She said, "You're only the second woman I know who walked away from the wrong guy to truly get God's choice."

I am *so* glad I did; so glad God gave me a tender enough heart to lay down what I thought was His will and surrender all my plans in exchange for His. I am, literally, stunned by the goodness of God!

When Cathy went to heaven, her family had to experience great pain and loss. Their spirits were crushed and many questioned God why it had to go that way.

I recognize their wounds and loss enabled restoration for me with Ross as my life partner. I am very aware God had provided the perfect husband for me through the loss of others.

I hear the stories. I try to connect with the great pain felt in the loss of a mother so beloved, a mother-in-law cherished, a one and only lover and wife of forty-nine years, an inspiration to many at The Summit. What a woman Cathy was. She loved her husband so much she encouraged him to marry again and quickly. She gave him a list. She knew him well after half of a century of love and relationship. She knew what he needed and what would make him happy. She let Ross know he would have her blessing if he chose to do so.

It was just three months after meeting me, and more than a year before she was diagnosed with cancer, that Cathy declared I was the one for him if anything ever happened to her. She also had lengthy conversations with her children, telling them not to give their father a hard time about remarrying. Was this prophetic? Did she somehow know, down deep, that God would take her?

I don't know. They knew Cathy had good discernment of character, so the transition was made easier, although there were ups and downs and emotions and struggles. But I do know God used those words and her list to bring peace in the family when He brought us together. Maybe she knew it would take her confirmation to bring closure, to bring peace and a sense of approval to the family and the church. Without such approval, division in a church body, or in a family, sometimes cannot be overcome.

God used Cathy Holtz to raise four children who have a strong sense of family and loyalty. Four children who love their Papa with a commitment rare these days. She left behind an unforgettable legacy of fierce love and quirky ways. Her memory lives on. I don't even try to fill her shoes for those who are left behind.

I honor her by loving those she loved the most . . . and by being me, the one she chose above the rest to take care of the one she loved so well.

FOURTEEN

The Desires of My Heart

There is no more lovely, friendly, and charming relationship, communion or company than a good marriage.

—Martin Luther

On June 13, 2014, I married my love, Ross Holtz.

The wedding was like a fairy tale for me. I had never had a big church wedding, and Ross wanted me to be happy.

"Darlin' Athena, whatever you want will plum tickle me to death," he said. "I'm willing to spend whatever we have to give you this gift."

He bought me an exquisite diamond ring from the local jeweler. Together we planned a beautiful wedding with 500 guests at The Summit. Our original date was going to be October or November, but Ross wanted to spend the summer with me and do some vacationing. We considered being married in a quiet office ceremony and keeping the June 13 date for the big shindig. Ross finally said, "No way. That would feel like we were lying to everyone and not sharing this amazing day."

On our wedding day I wore a simple, elegant, form-fitting but tasteful, long matte mesh gown with an empire bodice and lace cap sleeves, off-white with an open back. My friend Jessica and I had found it on the rack at a bridal store. It was a classic, stunning dress, and best of all for my budget, it was less than $200! I knew it was the one the moment I tried it on. I said, "Yes," to the dress, and the salesperson rang a bell, and the applause was thunderous throughout the store. Instead of a veil I chose a beautiful crème satin flowered headband.

We wanted to make a statement about what we believe at the wedding and whose we are (especially after my detour). Our entire family was involved in the bridal party and ceremony, except Roby, who was unable to travel from South Carolina. My firstborn, Ross's firstborn, and Ross's associate pastor of twenty-five years played "Creed" by Rich Mullins together to open the ceremony. Ross's firstborn officiated and did the hand binding while Ross's daughter put the clan ring on my finger and welcomed me into the Holtz Clan. After the beautiful ceremony, we enjoyed a scrumptious "potluck" hors d'oeuvres buffet and champagne, greeted friends joyfully, and danced the night away to the live music of The Hubcaps—with two of Ross's sons, Bret and Thad, playing in the band.

Although we had planned to slip away earlier, we were having so much fun dancing we finished the night with everyone else around midnight. Ross's motorhome was parked behind the historic Enumclaw landmark, the Field House, where we held the reception, so we didn't have far to go.

My wedding was a magical night, more than I ever could have hoped or dreamed for—a wonderful opportunity to put God and His faithfulness on display.

When I married Ross, I became Athena Dean Holtz, and a pastor's wife, and unknowingly entered a life of living in the proverbial ministry fishbowl.

While I said a wholehearted *Yes* to spending the rest of my life with this man, I had no idea what it meant to be a pastor's wife. I knew it would be refining, but I did not know what to expect.

"Sooo . . . what's it really like?" a friend cocked her head sideways and asked.

"Well . . . " I answered, not quite sure how to respond.

I am honored and humbled God would give me this man to love. Ross is a man whose heart is to proclaim God's faithfulness. His calling is vital, demanding, and rewarding, all at the same time. I do not take lightly the privilege of being his friend, confidante, fellow Jesus-follower, and lover.

From the moment we began to spend time together, believing God had brought us together with marriage as the goal, there were some highly charged reactions from some individuals we both thought were our friends. While Ross began grieving in June 2013 when Cathy's diagnosis of cancer first came, there were still some in the congregation who felt he was too easily replacing his wife of forty-nine years.

I do understand. Many who loved their pastor felt very protective of him. Understandably, emotions ran high. It wasn't long before we had people turning against us . . . some of whom had trusted Ross as their pastor for decades. It didn't seem to matter the entire family on both sides was supportive or that his late wife had encouraged him to remarry and put me on top of the list as potential spouses.

It was difficult, but ultimately rewarding, to watch him suffer betrayal and scorn from those he thought were his friends over his decision to marry me. I watched him grieve the losses and grow stronger. None of the people who left cited any sin issue. They just didn't like it, thought it disrespected Cathy, and didn't feel we were waiting long enough when we were married nine months after her death. Even though Cathy told him if he liked being married then he needed to remarry and quickly, and gave him "the list." Even with all the vocal blessing of his family and being chosen for him specifically by Cathy, there were hard feelings.

We lost three of the top five givers to the church and a whole gaggle of older single women who may have been mad they didn't have a chance with him.

Moving into the role of pastor's wife has required me to forgive, again and again, those who opposed my husband in one way or another regarding his decision to marry me. I know Jesus taught we must forgive seventy times seven. We all struggle with forgiving those who hurt us or those we love. As a regular churchgoer, it would be much easier to nurse a grudge and get away with it. But being the pastor's wife puts me in a fishbowl where everything I do and say is magnified, critiqued, and most times judged. I have no wiggle room . . . I must allow God to refine me through every challenge, every disappointment, every struggle, every betrayal.

James 3:1 talks about leaders and teachers being called to a higher standard. I believe this filters down to the pastor's wife. I joyfully accept the requirement because I want to see God do everything He wants to do through both of us and through the ministry He has established at The Summit.

So, what's it really like?

First, it's a blessing to be married to someone who is the same person on stage as he is at home. That makes our relationship authentic, which is so important to me. At the same time, I have a new level of the fear of the Lord. I realize my actions, emotions, decisions, and attitudes, good or bad, can affect a man who shepherds an entire congregation of believers. This is an intense responsibility I'm sure I haven't quite grasped in full.

I do struggle a bit with being in such a high-profile position during intimate times of worship. I often stand and raise my hands in surrender to God . . . and weep when something in a worship song or sermon touches my heart with gratefulness or conviction of sin. It's not hard for tears to flow when I'm worshipping. One time the enemy whispered, *If they see you crying, they'll wonder what's wrong.* I didn't listen then to this attempt to quench the moving of the Spirit in my life, and I won't in the future, although I know some may misunderstand.

This pastor's wife gig seems to be a test of my willingness to surrender in new ways.

Since I have a full-time commitment as a business owner, carving out time for us to spend together without one or the other of us working is quite an accomplishment. I have finally arranged my schedule to take Mondays off to spend the day with Ross. I typically want it to be downtime for him, so we do something restful and recreational. It's a Sabbath of sorts so his batteries are recharged.

Sometimes my well-laid plans just don't happen . . . someone lands in the hospital, a crisis comes up, we sense the need to visit someone who's homebound. Some evenings, hospital visits and other pastoral responsibilities take Ross's time. I could pout and whine, but instead, I have the opportunity to rejoice always and join him in the hospital visit or stay home and pray for the situation at hand.

It's just like any other marriage . . . you love one another, you nurture one another, you look for ways to encourage one another, and you lay down your lives for one another. Since it hasn't been three years yet since our wedding, it's hard to imagine neglecting one another or growing apart. Committing to building our relationship with God at the center makes all the difference.

I'm sure as we go along, I'll make mistakes and not meet people's expectations of what they think a pastor's wife should be. So, in advance, I continue to ask God to keep me sensitive to Him, open and real with my husband and our church family, and committed to His will in every area of my life.

I am experiencing true partnership in marriage for the first time. In my past, I was the breadwinner and often felt used for the money and lifestyle I could generate, while I used my ex-husband to care for the kids and avoid my family responsibilities. Really, we used each other.

In business, all my adult life I have been self-employed, usually the sole owner. I made unilateral decisions as I saw fit, rarely, if ever, asking for advice from my husband. I would just hire others to clean up any messes I left behind. The idea of partnership has been a new concept for me to learn with Ross. This has been such a huge change for me. He has helped me learn to lean on him for feedback, advice, wisdom for family relationship issues and business. And he does the same with me with church situations, challenges, and sermon input.

I am finding Ross is a perfect match for me—he is strong without being controlling—and thoughtful and deliberate in how he responds to situations. When I have been upset with a situation and want to tell the other person how he or she made me feel, he zooms out and helps me see what the ramifications might be if I were to follow through. He is over-the-top loyal and devoted to family and always focuses on helping me rebuild my relationships with those who were devastated by my bad choices.

In so many ways, we complete and complement each other with our personalities, in our relationship, and within the ministry.

I tend to be impulsive. He thinks and reasons before he jumps.

He can tend to be a bit of an Eeyore. I always see the glass half-full.

He is stable and educated and well respected. I admit I have been one who has made some very bad choices! He is the founding pastor and leader at The Summit, and I happily stand beside him to support and encourage.

I depend on Ross to be my anchor, to provide, which he does well, and to warn me when I am not thinking of possible ramifications of my attitudes. He is my rock and best friend. He helps me process my emotions when I feel hurt from something real or an imagined deed or thought by one of my kids, in-laws, or church members.

He depends on me for comfort, excitement, joy, exhortation and even to point out his blind spots. Companionship . . . doing things together or enjoying doing nothing together . . . is so important to him.

Ross cherishes me and encourages me and takes care of me. He is a gentleman and respectful and tender. We have yet to have a fight and are able to discuss disagreements with grace. And he loves to cuddle! We both have the same love language of physical touch and words of affirmation, which makes it so easy for us to show love to one another. He is also a very safe person who loves my company, even if it's just snuggling on the couch and being quiet.

Satan used inappropriate physical touch in my young life from the maid and worldly words of affirmation from my dad to send me off course. God brought me full circle to a husband with those same love languages expressed in godly ways to encourage me and allow me to feel loved in a healthy way by a man who adores me.

I am secure in his love for me; I don't feel a need to look for attention and acceptance elsewhere. He completes me.

I love our adventures together and making memories with family on the sailboat, on trips in the motorhome, and during holidays in our home. I love the companionship, even if it's just being in the same room reading; we simply enjoy each other's company.

We sharpen each other. He makes me want to be a better woman and wife. I make him want to be a better man. It's true—together we are better than the sum of our parts. I love doing things together, snuggling on the couch watching chick flicks, sitting next to him at church, going out to eat with him, watching the Seahawks, praying together. I love watching him preach and learning from him.

I love our little getaways in the motorhome, where we head out to places such as LaConner, Wash. right after church and park in the marina RV park, where we can walk into town, eat a lovely dinner, drink a little wine, share a delicious dessert, find some local music, or walk around town and window shop and then walk back to our little love nest and sleep in on Monday mornings. We have breakfast in town at our favorite spot, the Calico Kitchen and then spend a lazy day reading, or walking, or going to the tulip fields. Heading back home in the late afternoon, we feel refreshed and almost as if we took a longer vacation.

I love the give-and-take, the mutual respect and adoration. I love being nurtured and finding ways to bless my husband. I love dreaming together about adventures we will take, ideas for upgrading the house, taking a trip, or doing things together we've never done before.

We share favorite things with each other, reminiscing about our time of courtship and all God has done in our lives and how creatively He brought us together. My heart is happy!

FIFTEEN

A Redemption Story

Redeemed how I love to proclaim it, redeemed by the blood of the Lamb / redeemed through His infinite mercy, His child and forever I am.

—Frances J. Crosby

A few minutes before we were to do a ribbon-cutting ceremony to officially launch Redemption Press on April 1, 2014, I looked around, amazed at the restoration God had allowed. It was April Fool's Day and exactly four years after the ownership of WinePress had been transferred to the cult. City of Enumclaw officials, employees, friends and family, were all on hand to celebrate the launch of Redemption Press in my old publishing offices at 1730 Railroad Street in Enumclaw, Washington.

I never thought I'd be back in Washington. Way too many bad memories. Due to my own misjudgment of character, WinePress had fallen into the hands of leaders who were spiritually, emotionally, and financially abusive, arrogant, and elitist.

When WinePress closed its doors, the news made the nationally-distributed *Publisher's Weekly* on January 22, 2014 in an article entitled "Self-Publisher WinePress Goes Out of Business."

The company I had co-founded and had grown was no more. The money had flowed to the Williams family at the expense of the staff who were all loyal followers of Tim Williams and who gave all they had to serve there. Left in the wake of the closing of the company were the authors and former employees, many who had not been paid as promised. WinePress blamed its demise on "lies and gossip" and threatened to sue those who spoke out, but they couldn't keep the whole house of cards from folding.

With the closing of WinePress, nearly 2,000 authors became displaced, unable to get their hands on the books they'd paid to have produced and made available. Some 195 authors were in process—had paid for publishing services but never received what they paid for. With the company out of business, they had no hope of recovering their investment.

I was awed as I watched God turn something meant for evil into good.

WinePress owed Mike Reynolds, their landlord, a huge sum of money in back rent. They blamed me for not having the money to pay him and kept promising him they would pay.

Mike finally gave Tim Williams an ultimatum saying the only way he would let them stay in the buildings was if Tim put his name on the lease. When Tim refused, Mike sued them as tenants and was awarded a "landlord's lien" on all the assets in the office. Once he got the lien, he changed the locks and evicted WinePress. The publisher's property abandoned in the building was now considered the landlord's and could be sold to help pay the rent that was in arrears.

That's when I got the unexpected call in Texas from my friend, Jessica.

"Athena, would you consider coming back up to start a new company? It looks like Mike would be willing to let you use your old offices with all the furniture."

It turns out Mike felt badly about the many authors who had been "thrown under the bus" when he had to shut WinePress down. Instead of selling the furniture, computers, servers, etc., he offered to rent them to me so I could help the authors. Mike Reynolds has been a life saver in so many ways. Considering the huge financial hit he took from people I convinced him were worthy of taking over my business, he has bent over backwards to help me get back on my feet with Redemption Press. He has been incredibly flexible and has done everything possible to help me succeed. Another gift from God!

I consulted an attorney and got his opinion this was legal. Since Tim had not declared bankruptcy (I'm guessing because the trail would have led back to him even though his name was never on any paperwork), the assets were not in question. Anything once theirs was ours for the using.

After prayer and getting the legal go-ahead, it seemed like all the lights were green.

Kevin Cochran, the IT—information technology—guy for WinePress left the cult in December, just weeks before this came together. To help me, he was able to reverse Tim's attempt to wipe out all the data on the servers. He restored everything—the author files, the database of author names and contact and title information, along with the twenty-year old database of names and notes as to where authors had been in the writing or publishing process so we could contact them and help them take the next step. The many hours he spent helping me were without pay, and once again, another provision from God that made such a huge difference. I cannot imagine doing what we did to launch Redemption Press without his many hours of help and IT expertise.

Talk about a miracle! Had WinePress declared bankruptcy, the entire server with all the contents would have been considered assets and we would not have had any access. Instead, Tim Williams and his team just walked away and didn't continue paying what they owed.

The Quickbooks files I had access to showed Tim Williams taking his $20,000+ a month paycheck all the way up to closing the doors. This occurred while some employees were owed tens of thousands of dollars in back pay, two different printers were each owed over $50,000, and a huge list of editors had gone unpaid for months, not to mention all the authors who hadn't received any royalties for nearly a year. Then there were the authors in process who lost thousands upon thousands of dollars. All the while, Tim never had to wait for his enormous paychecks.

I named the new company, Redemption Press—a fitting name if ever there was one!

If it were not for the help of my friend, Jessica Gambill, the fledgling company never would have survived. Committed to assisting the abandoned authors with me, she helped me launch the new company from her living room and kitchen, as well as giving me a place to sleep in one of their upstairs bedrooms when I first came back.

While my budding romance and upcoming wedding plans kept my head in the clouds, Jessica worked diligently to keep the company afloat for the first nine months, giving us a good start.

Our first order of business was to send out an e-mail to all the WinePress authors letting them know the company had closed, but we were willing to do what we could to help them through Redemption Press.

In return, Tim Williams sent out a hateful e-mail to all the WinePress authors warning them I had all their credit card information, including their expiration dates and three-digit codes, everything I would need to illegally use them! He knew full well this information was all encrypted in the servers, and I had no way to get it, and was just trying to stop Redemption Press from going forward. While I'm sure it frightened some, most authors could see right through his fearmongering rhetoric.

We offered to return the files to the authors for no charge. If they wanted us to get them back into print under the new Redemption Press imprint, have the WinePress logo removed, get a new ISBN number, get the book uploaded and back into distribution, we offered those services for a nominal fee.

Enough authors were willing to take a chance on us in the first two months so we could pay the rent on a scaled-down version of my old offices, using only one side of the building. I lived in the apartment upstairs from April until our wedding date on June 13.

The landlord was thrilled to have someone who wanted the same configuration, needed the same desks, computers, furnishings, office supplies, etc. This was a complete answer to prayer. We had no start-up cash since my credit had been trashed, so we would have had no way to outfit the offices. Just to be able to start out with a month-to-month lease for the furnished offices was another miracle!

I never could have guessed I'd have the chance to help so many authors get back what was rightfully theirs, and at the same time, offer new a la carte solutions to publishing dilemmas to better serve authors.

I'm so thankful for the way God has already blessed Redemption Press. I'm proud of our personalized customer service and our commitment to coaching and advising each author and how this helps them end up with a professional, industry-standard product. I was thrilled when this was recognized by Mark Levine, in his sixth edition of *The Fine Print of Self-Publishing*. Redemption received the number one self-publisher rating, above other companies such as Xulon and Westbow. We don't publish thousands of books a year, as other custom publishers do who outsource work to third-world countries. Much of the work we do on manuscripts is done locally, and each manuscript is evaluated honestly. We take pride in our personal touch and our custom approach. Our authors are not taken advantage of but are valued by those who love Jesus and consider it a calling to walk out this publishing journey with the authors the Lord brings to Redemption Press.

God has turned my mourning into dancing and restored what I allowed the enemy to steal. He is redeeming every area of my life. He truly has given waters in the wilderness and rivers in the desert . . . and I can only praise Him for His goodness.

A Redemption Story

Because I provide water in the wilderness
and streams in the wasteland,
to give drink to my people, my chosen,
the people I formed for myself
that they may proclaim my praise.
(Isa. 43:20b–21)

SIXTEEN

In Process

I will repay you for the years the locusts have eaten—
. . . and you will praise the name of the Lord your God,
who has worked wonders for you.

—Joel 2:25–26

God has done so much to redeem and restore me, but some days are still hard.

I sat in church on Mother's Day listening to my husband speak on God's desire that we honor and respect our parents—especially our mothers—whether they deserve it or not.

This holiday, so special to many, is still hard for me. It isn't all happy and encouraging. It's bittersweet at best.

I have many regrets and have caused much wounding from my own inability to mother well. I struggle with knowing what to do with these feelings. I know I've been forgiven by God, but repentance is all about working through the consequences of my actions.

Growing up, my mom wasn't one who taught me the ways of God. And even though I gave my heart to Jesus at age thirty-three, I continued with my workaholic behavior for many years to come—denying the pain

I was masking by staying busy. My track record as a mother is marred by my own wounding and family of origin.

But, because God gave me the courage to look at myself and my own bad choices and sinful decisions, instead of pointing my finger at others and blaming them for my difficult circumstances, I repented and I began to heal and move on and grow. I learned from the discipline He brought into my life. He has brought life and redemption through His instruction. What I once viewed as correction has turned into a reward because He has used even this horrible experience in my life for the good, making it a perfect example of Romans 8:28. God wouldn't have done that if I'd chosen to grow bitter, blaming others or Him for my devastation and feeling sorry for myself.

As I listened to Ross speak, I realized I needed to honor my mom. I could honor the role she held in my life and appreciate her sacrifice, even though our relationship was never close, until the end. I thank God for the last months of her life when I had the privilege of helping care for her in Texas.

The truth is, families are messy. None of us is perfect. She let me down. I've let my kids down. More than once. She wounded me with her critical words and perfectionism, and I've wounded my children with my neglect and bad choices.

But as I sat listening to my husband on Mother's Day, I knew I could honor her for the sacrifice she made to mother me. I know it wasn't easy.

But Lord, my sins! How many they are. Oh, pardon them for the honor of your name. Where is the man who fears the Lord? God will teach him how to choose the best. He shall live within God's circle of blessing, and his children shall inherit the earth. Friendship with God is reserved for those who reverence him. With them alone he shares the secrets of his promises. My eyes are ever looking to the Lord for help, for he alone can rescue me.

(Ps. 25:11–15 TLB)

It's day four of a sailing adventure with the Holtz clan, and I am sitting on the bow of the thirty-foot *Tertian Quid*, the sailboat Ross has owned for about fourteen years, thinking about the faithfulness of God. And, unbelievable as it sounds, when Ross bought it, the boat was named *The Athena*. He changed the name of the boat, but the curtains on the inside still have my name—Athena—embroidered on each one of them!

It was as if they were waiting for me to come find them. God knows my name. He knows all about me. And He knew I would be sailing on this boat one day—a boat with my name embroidered on the curtains!

"Ross, what's the deal with the name of the boat?" I had asked when I first saw it.

"Ah, the Tertian Quid. It's a philosophy term, Athena."

"What does it mean, anyway?"

"It's a point between two polemics."

"That doesn't help," I said, inching closer to him.

Ross smiled and put his arm around me. "In the Greek mind, if you have law and grace, they couldn't touch. If they overlapped, one would diminish the other. The tertian quid is the mediating point. Jesus was the presentation of grace and the fulfillment of the law without diminishment of either one. Jesus was the mediating point. He was the tertian quid."

The Tertian Quid—I love how Ross saw the spiritual parallel in the philosophical term—the meeting of law and grace through Christ—just another example of God's grace in my life.

It was cool out on the water one early summer morning on what promised to be a hot day in Puget Sound. Bundled up in my sweatshirt, my fingers poked out of my sleeve to peck out the words on my laptop. Around me I saw the evidences of God's handiwork in everything. Everywhere I looked, His faithfulness and His goodness were so evident. I found myself asking Him all through the day, *What are You trying to teach me here?*

It wasn't always this way.

I'd have my quiet time in the morning and then just go on my way working, finding myself at the end of the day wondering where the time went. I usually couldn't recall one time during the day when I consciously thought about God. Then I'd feel so unspiritual . . . like a failure.

Those were the days of trying to live a life of spiritual perfection I'd been convinced was my duty. Condemnation loomed, the pressure to prove my repentance was real and my salvation deserved was choking the life out of me, and I didn't even know it.

In my devotions that morning, I had read words that expressed the truth I was missing in my days in the cult.

For God chose to save us through our Lord Jesus Christ, not to pour out his anger on us. Christ died for us so that, whether we are dead or alive when he returns, we can live with him forever. (1 Thess. 5:9)

God *chose* to save us. Nothing we did, or didn't do, changes this fact. He chose us, we didn't choose Him! He chose to save us rather than pour out his anger on us.

I had lived in a man-inflicted delusion that I had to constantly prove myself to Him. I had to check off my spiritual to-do list to show I was worthy of God's love and salvation. And the truth was, I couldn't do it. I couldn't prove I was good enough—because I wasn't and never would be. His grace is all I need. All I have to do is rely on His sacrifice and the blood He shed on my behalf. For this, I am so very thankful.

Every day I live this new life my gratefulness overflows. The farther I get from my former disabling legalism, the more my love for Christ fills my soul.

I don't *have to* try to stop and think of Him during my day . . . I can't help myself!

I will extol the Lord at all times; his praise will always be on my lips. I will glory in the Lord; let the afflicted hear and rejoice. Glorify the Lord with me; let us exalt his name together. (Ps. 34:1–3)

God is in the process of redeeming my relationships with my family.

My son Aaron was the first one I phoned when I woke up and decided to flee the cult. He was the only one of my children who kept trying. All my other kids were married with families and had rightfully moved on with their lives. From the time Aaron left the cult, he'd call over and over again, sometimes more than once a day. He'd stop by, trying whatever he could to get my attention. He was desperate to get me to see what I was doing.

After thorough brainwashing, I had believed he was the enemy and treated him as such, resulting in some deep wounds. Many of those wounds are still in the process of healing. Aaron was the one who took me to a lawyer who looked at the sale paperwork and proclaimed it fraud. Aaron was the one who got me to be willing to see the rest of my family and start the healing journey with Ailen.

Our relationship is a journey we're rebuilding, slowly. The effects of my being a workaholic neglectful mother, coupled with my eleven years of rejection, resulted in wounds that are still hard for him to handle, especially on Mother's Day and his birthday.

Ailen was the second one to accept me back and forgive me. God has totally restored our relationship. We now have a lunch date every two or three months. I enjoy his new wife, Olianna, and her children, Isaiah, Elisia, Haley, and Alexis. Ailen's children, Anna and Ezekiel, are again part of his life, and I am looking forward to even more restoration. They had been estranged from me since I left the cult and Malcolm Fraser was arrested. With slow steps, I'm beginning to reconnect with Anna. I was there when Anna was born while her mom and dad were in the cult. Now she is at least physically free from it, even though emotionally and mentally I think it's going to take some time.

Roby and I reconnected immediately when I walked away, but in person not until Thanksgiving of 2013 when I was in Texas. I never felt like much of a mother to her since she was eleven when Chuck and I married, and she was mostly out of the house with her mom and friends. But our relationship was built when she came back to live with us in the mid 90s. I took on a mother role with her and walked with her through major events and rejections in her life.

After our bonding, we went through two different "church" experiences where she experienced the trauma of my rejection. But there was a real sense of coming home when we physically reconnected mother to daughter in 2013. It has only grown since then, even though we live thousands of miles apart. I've gotten to know her two kids, Dante and Sophie, and am encouraged at how all those years ago, in the wake of the house church, God gave her Jeff as a husband, the perfect man for her! Roby and I have long catch-up conversations about God, family and life every few months or so. It is a blessing to be able to give her motherly advice—something I never thought I'd be any good at. He has given me words and instruction for her that have been an encouragement to her as well as to me.

Garrett was, understandably, very cautious and careful in rebuilding our relationship. After a particularly hurtful letter Tim Williams convinced me write to him, he distanced himself from me to avoid any further pain. Garrett and I were restored in March 2012 (three-and-a-half months after I walked away) and have worked through the forgiveness process with his pastor. The first year we reconnected by talking weekly, and slowly and deliberately trust was rebuilt, and I was welcomed into their family and named "Nuna"—their new grandma. Since then, I've visited many times with the whole family and God continues to restore my relationship with his wife, Tara, who saw through Tim Williams early on and put her foot down.

And then there's Chuck Dean, my ex-husband. When Chuck saw the way Sound Doctrine was going and wanted out of the church, I was counseled by Tim and Carla to fight against giving him anything at all from the business he co-founded.

When I came out of the cult I told him, "Chuck, I reaped what I sowed. I stole WinePress from you, and Tim Williams stole it from me. I was so wrong to do that to you. I am sorry. Would you please forgive me?" It took a few months for him to process this and fully forgive me, but he did.

I felt I should give Chuck a "founder's royalty" from Redemption Press, 1 percent per month, as my restitution. When he walked away from WinePress, in our divorce he asked for $800 a month for life (which we fought him on and did not allow him to receive). Amazingly, $800 a month back then in 2000, was exactly 1 percent of the WinePress revenues. Chuck's experience with Tim Williams strongly contributed to his walking away from God, so I continue to pray for him to return.

SEVENTEEN

Coming Home

My people will live in peaceful dwelling places, in secure homes, in undisturbed places of rest.

—Isaiah 32:18

As the Lord began restoring me, He used the physical settings He placed me in to speak to me of my place in Him, in His family, and in His kingdom.

I felt most at home as a child in my grandmother's old house overlooking the beach in Santa Monica, which had once belonged to Mary Pickford.

When I was a teen, we had a beautiful million-dollar home with an indoor pool, but the house didn't matter to me. I was never a homebody; I preferred to be out riding my horses or running around with my friends.

I've lived in a beautiful house on Silver Lake in Los Angeles, a new home with a barn in Burbank, and a Tudor-style house in Bothell, Wash.

While in multi-level marketing, the view of the blue waters of Puget Sound and the snow-topped Olympic mountain range from our Mukilteo two-story contemporary was phenomenal. Excited about all the money rolling in, I ordered all new furniture and filled the house with dark wood furniture and fabrics in rich jewel tones.

We lived first in a log cabin when we moved to Enumclaw. Then, when we planned to move Tim Williams and his family out to Washington, we purchased a beautiful sandstone 1940s home originally built for the owner of the Wilkinson Sandstone Quarry. It had lots of character, and knotty pine walls throughout the finished basement where we envisioned church gatherings and sweet fellowship. The living room upstairs had curved alcoves to the adjoining hall and dining room and was a perfect setting for Sunday afternoon services when we started out. I upgraded the kitchen appliances, redid the kitchen floor, and the master bath, and converted the garage into a beautiful office. As I was sinking money into the renovation of the house, I thought, *This is all going to be used for God.*

I didn't have a place to live after leaving Sound Doctrine and WinePress. Having alienated myself from my family, there were no options there. Scrambling to find work to support myself, I had no idea where I would live. For almost seven months I was basically homeless, staying with friends.

"I found you a house!" my friend, Jessica, said on the phone.

A few hours earlier she had noticed a For Rent sign up in front of her all-time favorite house in Enumclaw. She had often driven by the house and admired the improvements the owner had made, wishing someone she knew could live there. I quickly called the number she gave me and left a message.

It wasn't long before I got a call back and a woman's voice on the other end of the phone told me I was the second person to leave a message. "I wasn't going to call anyone back until the evening, but I felt compelled to call you."

"Can I share a bit of my story with you?"

After I told her what I was coming out from she said, "If you want the place, it's yours. I won't call anyone else back, and I'll take the sign down right away."

I hadn't even seen the inside of the house yet! I told her, "I can tell just by seeing the outside that I will be happy with the inside."

I simply felt the hand of God all over the situation. We agreed to meet on Sunday morning before church so I could see the inside of the house. When Jessica and I went over to meet the owner and take a look, it was just like visiting with a long-time friend. The owner had moved into the house during a traumatic transition time in her own life and had created a sanctuary out of it.

"I can see it's the perfect place for you with everything you've been through."

It felt very much as if God had set it up and orchestrated all the details.

As we chatted I said, "I'll be furnishing it a little at a time." Laughing, I added, "I don't have any furniture or anything . . ."

"Well, do you like what's here? I can let you use whatever you would like." Honestly, I felt lightheaded and almost at a loss for words. *The house was decorated exactly as I would decorate a house if money were not an issue*—from the colors, the furniture, the lighting fixtures, everything down to the smallest details.

We went on from there to church and then back again to meet with her to work out all the details. I was stunned at God's goodness. To say

God had provided for me would be an understatement. Later that week, I moved all my earthly possessions—mostly clothes and books—into what felt like a bed and breakfast, a beautiful sanctuary, a place of rest. The master bedroom had French doors opening onto a small pond with a waterfall and lush garden blooming with beautiful flowers. It truly was surreal. The Lord was restoring to me a sense of home with the gift of these elegant and beautiful surroundings.

The house brought such refreshment to my soul. After a time, I filled my new office with all new dark wood furniture. The sense of favor and love I felt from Jesus was stunning.

When it was time for me to go help my brother take care of my mom in San Antonio, I moved into Jim's two-bedroom-plus-den rental in a quiet, tree-lined neighborhood. I guess it was Momma's house as her social security check paid for it. Jim had sold her townhouse in Glenview, Ill. and moved her and all the necessary furnishings down to Texas. Although it wasn't a spacious house, it had many memories of my family life displayed throughout, furniture I grew up with, and photos and mementos.

The first time I went to Ross's house was for the 2014 Super Bowl when the Seahawks were playing. The house is 100 years old, and with its exposed, old-growth straight-grain fir beams, is full of character, something I have always loved. I looked around at rooms filled with warmth and laughter, family, and chaos. Mementos of life and photos of Cathy and the grandkids were scattered across the walls, and the bookcases were filled with old books, giving a rich feel to the house.

The den that had become a storage room over the years had already begun its makeover. Ross had made it his room after Cathy passed. He picked a brick red for all four walls and two different shades of cream for the crown molding and ceiling. He had the built-in drawers rebuilt. How did he know I would have picked the same color paint for the walls? But God knew! I was delighted to discover Ross's tastes were so similar to mine.

I am home now in a house Ross has lived in for thirty years, but I am making it mine.

I laugh when I remember worrying I would end up with a guy with bad taste in clothes or furnishings.

It's amazing how God prepared me for this marriage. After losing everything I owned, it was simple for me to move into Ross's world. My kids were spread out all over; I didn't own a house anymore or any furniture. Joining the Holtz Clan and making my place by Ross's side in his world was a natural thing.

When I moved in, I wanted to honor Cathy's memory and give the grandchildren a chance to continue grieving without making any sudden changes. They all knew their Nona had picked me out for their Papa, but I felt strongly it would be good to wait a year before changing anything. So, for the first year, that's what I did.

Our first Christmas, I just put my family pictures on the bookcase to the left of the fireplace and positioned all Ross's family pictures on the right. Up in the window above the bookcase sits the beautiful memorial blown-glass piece containing some of Cathy's ashes next to a picture of her with her granddaughters. It had been in a prominent place on the mantle. After a year, I moved it next to the pictures on the bookcase, still in a prominent place.

After a year, I began to add some decorative items to the mantle, the dining room table, and the piano top. I added ceiling fans to the living room and bedroom. New throw pillows on the couches, all with the brick red, dark sage, and gold color scheme brightened the room. On our second Thanksgiving and Christmas together, I picked my own dinnerware, a combination of dark red, sage, and mustard-yellow dinner settings with muted gold tablecloths.

A big change was choosing my own decorations for the Christmas tree, rather than the ones they'd used for decades. When I first visited the house, I noticed the tall, skinny, artificial pine tree in the corner with white lights on it. It had become their tradition to keep the tree up all year. After our second Christmas together, I did the same—left the tree up all year. The gold and red theme matched the living room décor and I love seeing the twinkly lights all year!

Eventually we will redo the kitchen into something more to my liking, another opportunity to make the house mine.

I've seen and heard horror stories where a controlling and domineering new wife took her husband away from his world and made him join hers, or the new wife who demanded the husband's family be cut off. Or wives who showed no care, sensitivity, or diplomacy with the adult children. I was determined to fit in to Ross and his family's world, while still making a place for myself.

I am blown away at how carefully the Lord led us through the transition to respect the grieving of those who'd lost their mom, Nona, and mother-in-law. God helped me to be sensitive to this in many ways.

My transition to feeling at home was not without struggle. It took a while before it felt like mine. Ross's youngest son and his family had moved in right after Cathy went to heaven. Much of the cleaning out of Cathy's things was done before I moved in, but we were newlyweds sharing the house with two lively kiddos under the age of five, and two adults who were not only grieving the loss of their mom/mother-in-law, but who were also struggling to keep their marriage alive.

Much later, they said they expected Ross to remain single so all his focus could be on helping them save their marriage.

Our bedroom was the only part of the house I could call ours alone—but it had no place to sit or study or write. In the early days, in my frustration with all the chaos in the house, I often sought refuge in taking long showers where I'd weep and pour out my heart to God.

I felt unable to speak into my new stepson's or daughter-in-law's life as I barely knew them. I felt as if I was an unwelcome addition and poor replacement for Cathy who was exceptional with kids.

Cathy was the opposite of me—a stay-at-home mom for their entire marriage; she was highly involved in child care, home schooling, and children's ministry. I, on the other hand, just simply seemed to lack mothering aptitude. I only knew how to keep occupied with my work and be successful in that area.

I remember one time in my early days at The Summit when Cathy said to me, "I hate you!" with smiling eyes and a giggle.

Wide-eyed I stared at her with a huge question mark across my face.

"You get to do such cool stuff in business, and all I've ever done is take care of kids!"

It was true, but I felt it was more to my shame!

Cathy and I were very different, which has been an adjustment for everyone.

It was a big change for the congregation to see me sitting next to Ross in services. Cathy never sat with him in worship services. She chose to be in the back or helping at children's church. Since we announced our engagement, I have attended both the Saturday night and Sunday morning service sitting next to Ross on the front row.

Cathy never felt competent as a pastor's wife, so her experience wasn't as enjoyable as it could have been. Ross was protective of her and didn't ask her to be "up front."

I knew I would be involved in church activities, but after the women's ministry pastor passed away three days after our wedding, we both knew it would only be a matter of time before I'd have the bull's-eye on my back to be involved, as if I didn't already!

We brought different gifts to the table. One thing I enjoy has been different for Ross. I love hospitality and want to open our home to those in the church. Cathy saw her home as a refuge from the storms of ministry life. I try to keep the house ready so people can come by and feel welcomed at any time.

Besides feeling in the shadow of Ross's wife of forty-nine years, for the first seven months of our marriage, I walked on eggshells around his family and relegated the house to my new daughter-in-law. I found my refuge in the motorhome parked in back where I could escape to have some peace and quiet. There, I'd read and write, and Ross and I would share quiet time alone.

During this time of struggle and refining for me, I would grumble at times about the mess in the house. Then God brought to mind: *I clean up your messes don't I?* I had to learn to let the chaos be a prompt to pray rather than resenting it. But often I felt as if I wasn't handling my early days in the new house well.

I had always processed my pain and struggles out loud and in public—on my blog and on Facebook— which is no longer an option for me. Living in the pastor's wife fishbowl, I had to deal with my struggles in other ways. The privacy of a good cry in my shower and writing out my feelings in my journals became safe havens. I also developed friendships with other pastors' wives and processed my adjustments with them.

Eventually, after thirteen-and-a-half months of me learning to extend extra grace to them, his son and daughter-in-law and children moved out, and we had the house to ourselves.

Ross, as head of the clan, enjoys having his family around. He never wants anyone to feel left out, and it seems everyone wants to be part of the Holtz clan!

I am learning to let go of trying to have everything be perfect. I am finding out things won't always turn out like I expect but will always work for my good.

My emotions are still raw when it comes to building new family traditions with the blending of our families. I want things to go a certain way, and when they don't, it feels like I'm still being punished for my bad choices. I am then tempted to feel painfully mistreated. But then God does way beyond whatever I could have asked and makes a way better memory than I could have orchestrated!

This holiday season of 2016, it felt strange having Christmas and New Year's land on Sundays, work days for Ross. The holiday was somewhat disjointed as some of the family were spending Christmas with in-laws, so everyone would not be together at one time.

Then I felt like I was being relegated the leftovers of time with my firstborn son and daughter-in-law who were driving up from California to her folks' house a few hours north of here. We were to have one late evening and morning with them a few days before Christmas weekend at the end of their twelve-hour drive.

I felt hurt and discouraged and had a hard time shaking it. I was allowing self-pity to rule and could not see how anything good could come of it.

After pouring my heart out to God, I asked Him for a change of heart, a different perspective. I then began to thank Him for the time we *would* have together. His peace washed over me, and my heart embraced the opportunity to make the most of our time together.

I began inviting all our other family members over for a late Thursday night dinner. The house was full of laughter and chaos as twenty-three people ate Chinese food together, played games, and opened gifts.

Initially, I wanted a full-blown sit-down dinner with my momma's signature dish—flank steak marinated in soy sauce, honey, mustard, and garlic. Along with that, her famous burned butter rice, and butter-glazed carrots. I wanted tablecloths, a beautiful centerpiece, and good dishes to grace the table. But with twenty-three people coming, I quickly realized this wasn't the best idea. Aaron suggested Chinese food, and it was full-on, take-out chopstick madness at the Holtz Clan home!

The added kiss on the cheek from God was being able to have my granddaughter, Anna, with us to spend the night with the rest of her stepsisters and go tubing in the mountains with the family the next day.

So often God has a different idea than mine, which is so much better. When I'm in the thick of my discouragement, it's just so hard to see it! Ross has been amazing as he helps me see the opportunity for making a memory, rather than wallowing in self-pity when life's not going as I expected.

EIGHTEEN

Full Circle

We know we're coming full circle with God when we stand at a very similar crossroad where we made such a mess of life before, but this time we take a different road.

—Beth Moore

God is so good to surprise us with full-circle moments.

I had a little dream of getting my husband away for a week of total relaxation. We had planned to spend two more weeks in August on the sailboat, but that was not always relaxing for him. A thirty-year old sailboat often needs work, as something is always breaking and needing repair.

We'd also just spent a month in the middle of a family storm causing some emotional stress. When I saw an offer for a last-minute cruise, I thought, *This is a good way to decompress, relax and allow the Lord some space to do His work in our hearts.* It just felt like the right thing to do. I had been on cruises before, but most of them had been work related. This would be different—no seminars to run, no details, or schedules to manage.

I visited a website for steep-discount "last minute cruises." I started searching with some specific criteria:

- It had to leave from and return to Seattle (no time or money to fly to Florida to get on a boat!).
- The stateroom had to have a balcony.
- It had to be at least 50 percent off or more.
- Sailing date had to be the second or third week of August.
- It had to leave on a Sunday.

Finally, I nailed down an option with a great price, and all the other aspects were in order. I booked the cruise and went on with my day.

As our departure date approached, I began thinking about my past experiences on cruises.

While I was in the middle of my detour into deception, I had the idea to do a writer's cruise as a special event for the Northwest Christian Writer's Association (NCWA), where I was in leadership at the time. Over the next six years, we held three NCWA Alaskan Christian writer's cruises, each time bringing in a keynote speaker, editors, and other industry professionals. They were wonderful events, but there was always tension going on behind the scenes because Tim was ultimately in charge.

Tim Williams decided (after getting a taste of the good life) to take the staff of WinePress on another cruise to further exert his authority as management and move his agenda forward. The focus on the cruise was convincing us all (but most importantly me) that raising the rates for WinePress services was doing God's will because this was His business. Any of us who had reservations about the new prices he was setting were "in sin."

I had frequently complained about the inflated prices and the diminishing value provided for the services being sold. I had not built the company on those principles. The price increases bothered me, as I felt we would be taking advantage of people. When I voiced my opinion, I was in trouble and was told I was in rebellion against God's will. All along, it was all about him lining his pockets—it had nothing at all to do with God's will.

I thought about how different my life was now, getting ready to go on another cruise—this time with the love of my life, my new husband. No more undertones, manipulation, games, and humiliation.

I had forgotten the details of when we had gone on the earlier cruise but was beginning to put the pieces together. When I looked at the pictures of the ship, I realized the ship we were booked on was the same ship we sailed on with the WinePress cruise.

Calling the cruise line, I told the representative I'd been on their ships in the past and had an upcoming trip booked. "Could you look me up and tell me when I was on the boat last?"

"Yes, I found you," the rep said. "Your roommate was Jan Owens, and you sailed on August 24, 2008 on the Norwegian Pearl."

I almost dropped the phone.

Our tickets for the cruise were from August 16 to August 23, exactly seven years later. On the same ship. To the same place.

Oh. My. I smiled a huge smile. How gracious is the love of God! He can redeem even a cruise where He loves to show off His magnificence in nature and provide rest and relaxation for weary souls.

Seven is the biblical number of completeness and perfection (both physical and spiritual). Biblestudy.org says it derives much of its meaning from being tied directly to God's creation of all things.

Seven years earlier, the former cruise had been used by the evil one as part of the plan to destroy my soul and condemn me into silent submission. But here I was, about to embark on the same ship, this time with the man of my dreams, free from the chains of spiritual abuse, legalism, and deception . . . to be refreshed and renewed . . . to have this experience the way a gracious God would have it, not the counterfeit I had experienced in the past.

Redemption! It takes my breath away. God truly is faithful. Always.

I have come home to so many things—myself—a healthy relationship with God—new love—my family—a new home—restoration of my business and ministry—and ultimately the faithfulness of God. Of course, I have not arrived—that's obvious! I learn new lessons daily.

As a child, I watched my mom who never wanted to rock the boat and just ignored conflict and pretended it wasn't there. In dealing with church and family conflict and drama, I am learning to calm the conflict and ditch the drama.

Since my early days of marriage included domestic violence as an almost daily occurrence, I've stayed away as much as possible from toxic drama and outbursts of anger. But now conflict seems to be something God wants to help me deal with in a healthy way.

If I stand for truth, I certainly can't just be in denial and pretend a situation is not happening. While I can't control how someone else acts, I can control how I respond. I am learning to respond with compassion, understanding, gently, yet firmly—in my house, office, and in our church. Rather than to run from conflict or deny it, I need to acknowledge it and have some clearly defined expectations.

What a blessing and revelation it has been to address conflict and disagreements in our marriage in a healthy way. We *have* had a few issues we viewed very differently, but airing them has never turned into fights. As mature adults, we've processed our feelings and thoughts and came away with a resolution. It's so encouraging to me when we are able treat one another with respect and honor, even when we don't agree.

The truth is I am still a recovering Pharisee! Learning to grab on to grace and avoid judgmentalism is a daily journey. My twelve years of being influenced by a leader who pointed the finger at others and angrily accused them of disobeying Scripture, being sinful, being on the wide road while he was on the narrow road, and being selfish and greedy. While accusing others, he was the one who was all those things himself.

As I began to be washed clean of the error of my thinking and deprogrammed of all the lies I believed, a friend gave me a good suggestion.

"Whenever you have a thought that accuses someone of sin, or seems judgmental, simply ask the Holy Spirit "What do *you* say?"

I find this so helpful. The first time I attended church at The Summit, the worship leader at the time was leading worship in bare feet. Of course, the judgmental thoughts came spewing into my mind, "How dare she be so irreverent!" As I asked the Holy Spirit to show me what He saw, I remembered how David took off his robe and danced before the Lord and how Moses took off his shoes as he stood on holy ground. Bam! Judgmental thought obliterated!

Another time I was feeling condemned for the blessing of the rental house the Lord gave me after I left the cult. Beautifully decorated and fully furnished, it felt like an amazing kiss on the cheek from my Savior. I knew the cult leaders would be thinking and saying this was from Satan made to "look like" a gift from God to keep me believing a lie.

Before I let that thought get burrowed too far into my heart, I asked the Holy Spirit, "What do you say?" Immediately the Scripture came to my mind, "Woe to those who call good evil and evil good" (Isa. 5:20). Boom! Lie from the pit of hell obliterated.

Years later, the Lord still answers my "show-me prayer," even when I don't ask for it.

One time, I was being very judgmental about how much grace Ross was giving his youngest son when I clearly felt it was undeserved. Within moments, the Lord dropped this into my mind: *What if it were your youngest son? How would you respond?*

He knew the answer. I would show him grace and unconditional love—even if I didn't think he *deserved* it.

God is so faithful to speak to me and set me straight.

I was indignant about how wrong it was for someone to hold a grudge against me. No sooner had I railed in my mind against this person, the Lord gently showed me how I was also holding a grudge against him. Conviction washed over me and turned my bony finger of accusation into an upturned face with tears of repentance.

Over and over, when I point out how someone else is in the wrong, God gently reminds me of my need for Him by showing me my own heart. Thank God for His faithfulness and underserved grace and mercy!

I've never seen myself as a fearful person, but more of a risk taker and fearless type of individual.

September 2015, I felt like I was supposed to host a Bible study using Grace Fox's study, *Moving from Fear to Freedom.* At first I thought, *I know there are some other ladies who could benefit from the study.* I made plans to host it in my home more as a blessing to them.

Funny how God likes to make sure I eat a little humble pie every now and again. Right before the Bible study started, I had a storm blow into my life that left me fearful of the future. It was the familiar old bugaboo—finances!

I was having a major cash flow crunch at Redemption Press. We were thousands in the red, which meant, not only could I obviously not take a paycheck, but neither did I have the money to pay for my radio time for Always Faithful Radio. This was such a huge drop in cash flow I feared God was closing the door on the press or on my radio ministry.

Those old cult-inspired thoughts tried to creep in about sin and consequences.

Am I in sin? Is God punishing me? Is this an attack from the enemy to distract me from putting my attention on our women's retreat less than a week away?

All day long my mind was preoccupied with the storm and the what-ifs, and the what-should-I-do thoughts.

- *What if the worst happens?*
- *How will I navigate this?*
- *Will I survive it?*

- *Will I have to let some ministry commitments go because the funds aren't there to cover them?*
- *Am I in sin? Did I do something to cause the storm?*

Fear consumed me and left me incapable of being present for anyone. I tried to work. I had e-mails to write, face-to-face meetings, phone calls to make, details of the publishing company to address. But my mind was somewhere else. I feared the worst.

I knew I needed to face my fear and learn to trust God in new ways. When I returned home after work to Ross, I was an emotional wreck. Weepy, insecure, fearful. I needed my husband to hold me and protect me from the storm.

Ross gently reminded me of a circumstance just a week or two earlier when finances at the church left him wondering if he'd get paid that week. We recalled together how the conversation went. We'd had a lively debate about God's faithfulness and His promises to provide what we need. I had glibly challenged him with a forthright, "Just trust God!" My choleric personality and lack of compassion created an admonishment to him that wasn't especially encouraging.

Now the tables were turned, and I needed an understanding ear. Ouch!

If Ross had taken my approach, he'd have exhorted me, "God is always faithful, so just trust Him with the details!"

Thank God, Ross is not at all like me! True to form, he responded with compassion and wisdom. He helped me process through the steps I needed to take to face the storm instead of attempting to deny it or run from it. He held me as I wept, and he empathized with my fears. He didn't just give me pat answers or trite advice.

This set me back on a path of actively, intentionally trusting God, and accepting His provisions—*or His lack thereof.* I was encouraged to remember God's goodness and faithfulness regardless of what the outcome looked like to me.

When the ladies came over for the Bible study on fear I knew God was speaking directly to my own heart as we read these verses together.

> I prayed to the LORD, and he answered me.
> freeing me from all my fears.
> Those who look to him for help will be radiant with joy;
> no shadow of shame will darken their faces.
> I cried out to the Lord in my suffering, and he heard me;
> He set me free from all my fears.
> For the angel of the LORD guards all who fear him;
> and he rescues them.
>
> (Ps. 34:4–7)

What happened to my circumstances?

God gave me a new perspective as I shifted my focus and priorities to follow up with authors the Lord had sent to us who needed to be encouraged. By early October, our cash flow eased up. Even though there wasn't enough for me to get paid until November, we were back in the black in October.

God provided!

Sometimes my hard times—and the times I fear—are times of instruction, sometimes they are correction. At first I freaked out, not trusting God would provide. I had something to learn, even though I had gone into the study thinking I wasn't a person who struggled with fear.

God has indeed rescued me, redeemed my life, forgiven me, and He continues to make all things work together for good. Through it all, He has been faithful. His grace is greater than all my sin. His kindness has drawn me in. He has given me victory over the enemy of my soul. His love has never given up on me.

I noticed in Psalm 34:7, God seems to replace one type of fear with another. *Out* with the fear defined as a distressing emotion aroused by impending danger, evil, pain, etc. *In* with the fear of the Lord, defined as a reverential awe.

The angel of the Lord guards *all* who fear Him. That big, burly, strong, holy, righteous angel of the Lord stands before us, guarding our hearts—our mind, will, and emotions. Fear, on the other hand, wreaks havoc and sets us down a wrong path. But because we fear Him, the angel of the Lord guards us.

Thank the Lord, as we pray to Him, He answers us and frees us from all our fears. I trust I will never stop thanking the Lord for His faithfulness, goodness, compassion, and grace in my life.

After my return to Seattle I enjoyed a few months of successful radio ministry on KGNW, sister station to KSLR in San Antonio, yet I felt led to take a year's sabbatical to focus on my new role as a wife.

After a year off to get used to being married again and adjusting to the life of a pastor's wife, God opened up a new door for me to walk through on another station. Always Faithful was invited to air on AM 630 KCIS. Notice anything familiar? Talk about a full circle! I started on AM 630 KSLR in San Antonio in 2013. I was asked to relaunch the show in August of 2015 on the CRISTA Ministry station in the Seattle market (no relation to the Texas station). When I walked back into the radio studios on the beautiful CRISTA campus, it felt like home as I had been interviewed on KCIS many times over the past thirty years.

I never grow weary of affirming the faithfulness of God on the air. While I'm not doing a no-host lunch afterwards as I did in Texas, I enjoy connecting with my listeners at county fairs and other public venues. When people stop by the Always Faithful Radio booth I interview them and hear their stories of how God has been faithful in their lives and put segments on the air.

A highlight last fall was being able to minister to the young man from the booth next to ours who had been raised by an outspoken atheist. When he started hanging out in our booth, asking questions about God, I shared with him what God has done in my life. A few hours later, I had just the right guy to talk with him—my husband!

It's amazing to watch the challenges that come with radio ministry. I always know when we are on topics challenging to the enemy's lies in believer's lives—our technology challenges get ridiculous. Audio recordings vanish. Wireless connections fail. When my guests address suicide, depression, trauma or abuse, this gets especially pervasive and lets me know we are on the right track. After all, isn't the enemy of our souls named the *prince of the power of the air*? He will certainly go all out to attempt to hinder the truth of God from being proclaimed over the airwaves.

When my schedule is overfull and I feel like I am spinning too many plates in the air, I consider letting the radio ministry go, but it seems God just won't let me. This plate brings with it challenges with technology, guest bookings, as well as the financial commitment, but He continues to bless the ministry and encourage me as I encourage women.

Radio gives me a platform to share the lives of those with a testimony of God's faithfulness amid the trauma and trials of life. I love introducing my listeners to women who may be well-known or obscure but who share the same passion for others to know they are not alone in their suffering. Together we share the truth of God's faithfulness, even when we are in pain or the depths of despair.

It always encourages me to see raw and real stories come across my desk, written by women who are not trying to look all put together. As I've interviewed those who've experienced the many aspects of brokenness, they've all proclaimed the same truth: in the pain of life, Jesus meets us and draws us to Himself.

Recently I interviewed Esther Fleece, who is recognized among *Christianity Today's* "Top 50 Women Shaping the Church and Culture" and CNN's "Five Women in Religion to Watch." Her new book *No More Faking Fine: Ending the Pretending* caught my eye among all the other titles presented to me for potential interviews. She shared her wisdom and insight into the blessing of embracing the pain, known in Scripture as the "lament"—a gut-level act of giving a voice to your brokenness as you pour your heart out to God. I identified with Esther, as she too used work and success to numb the pain shoved down deep.

I also had a wonderful conversation on the air with Tina Samples, co-author of *Wounded Women of the Bible: Finding Hope When Life Hurts.* Her study is of little-known women in Scripture who share the same wounds as we do of imploding relationships, incapacitating losses, injurious personal mistakes, or spiritual failures. Realizing we are not alone is key in gaining the courage to surround ourselves with others who are walking their healing journeys. We need each other!

Then there is Grammy-award-winning singer/songwriter Laura Story who shared from her second book, *When God Doesn't Fix It: Lessons You Never Wanted to Learn, Truths You Can't Live Without.* Hers is a rich story of facing life with the anguish of her husband's brain tumor, while caring for young children and serving God in a vibrant music ministry. Her experiences in taking her broken dreams to God and trusting Him to work all things together for the good shows us the healthy way to process the death of a dream.

One of my all-time favorite interviews was with Michele Pillar who wrote *Untangled: The Truth Shall Set You Free.* God allowed her celebrity life as a contemporary Christian music artist in the 80s and 90s to crash and burn, only to redeem it by healing and untangling the emotional scars from a teenage abortion, affair, broken marriage, and many other traumas.

There are so many examples of powerful stories and insights from women who've struggled with depression, fear, anxiety, abuse, shame, loss, or grief. Through the dark night of the soul, the painful waiting for His healing, these women have all emerged strengthened with a new depth of insight and compassion. God has met them in the middle of the refining work of suffering in their lives.

What a full circle time it is when I can rejoice with other women who, like me, have known the depths of despair but have also experienced God's restoration of the joy of their salvation.

I have also come full circle to being back in fellowship with the Northwest Christian Writer's Association, a ministry I feel strongly about. I've even moved into the role of president for 2016-2017. I was president of the organization once before Tim Williams in 2005 attempted to silence me by telling me I "couldn't be trusted" to serve another year. I stepped down to a different position until 2009 when he determined I wasn't pleasing to God because I hadn't done something he wanted. My privilege to serve in leadership there, or even attend meetings, was revoked. The same happened with the International Christian Retail Show (ICRS) where I always represented WinePress, as well as various writer's conferences. If I was in trouble for not being a loyal follower, Tim cut me off from public appearances of any kind.

When friends asked, "Where's Athena?" at the writer's group or the conferences, they'd be answered by Carla or another staff member on the approved list, with a vague statement of how I was busy with other things. No one knew what I was going through at the time.

With the presidency has come a greater level of responsibility with the board meetings, monthly meetings an hour north, and our annual writers' renewal. This was an area where I had to be willing to say, "If we don't have a volunteer for the position then the job doesn't get done." This is a difficult thing to say for someone who wants to see professionalism displayed at all levels of the organization. As I have trusted Him with this spinning plate, He has increased our numbers and orchestrated a great team of writers committed to helping others grow in their craft.

With multiple plates spinning in the air at one time, I lean on God's promise: "My grace is sufficient for you for my power is made perfect in weakness. Therefore I will boast all the more gladly about my weaknesses, so that Christ's power may rest on me" (2 Cor. 12:9).

My ministry to my husband is at the top of my list. Praise God, he is a pretty independent guy and doesn't need an enormous amount of attention and is not at all demanding. It is a delight to spend my evenings with him. I do my best to guard our time off on Mondays so we can feed our relationship and keep it fresh.

The plate with my family's name on it is my next priority. This one spins evenly, especially since they are all adult children and not high maintenance. The Lord has been orchestrating divine appointments for memory making with them and my grandchildren. I'm learning to fan the flame of family times that grow and nurture relationships, thanks to the example of the Holtz family.

I still feel the very real and deep emotion that comes along with the wounding and healing God is bringing in my family. This requires more thoughtful and prayerful processing, which Ross is also helping me walk me through.

Since June of 2015 I've been co-leading the women's ministry at The Summit, along with the associate pastor's wife, Debbie Streuli, most specifically the monthly gatherings called Women of the Word (WOW). I'd love to have more time to spend on this, but I ask God to help me do the best I can and trust Him to do the rest through others. What a challenge for a recovering perfectionist! It has been a time of watching God work despite my limited amount of emotional bandwidth and time to devote to the ministry.

Then there's my call to write and speak about the faithfulness of God that is finding expression through the thoughts in this book.

I had an amazing full-circle moment when I remembered the Lord's call, way back in 1997, to equip the body of Christ. I felt strongly He wanted me to share insights into the parallels of warfare and Satan's strategies, along with helping women heal from their own post-traumatic stress disorder. The call came not very long before we, as a family, stepped into deception by publishing the book for Tim Williams. Thus began the dismantling of WinePress Publishing, my ministry, my marriage and our family.

It seems almost daily I'm reminded how I need to battle daily against the unholy realm that seeks to stir up disappointments, gossip, suspicions, false accusations, deception, conflict, division, offense, anger, upheaval, grudges, resentfulness, hypocrisy, and bitterness. I need to be aware of this in the church, in the publishing company, in our family, our relationships, and in our ministries.

This involves continual forgiveness of those who've hurt my feelings, offended me, and even those who hate me and continue to believe the lies of Tim Williams. I am learning to pray for them in a new measure and with a different heart. As well as spending quality time in prayer, I have come to the realization we must daily—and verbally—put on the armor of God and actively resist the work of Satan.

I was a near casualty of the enemy's strategies. I've learned the importance of being aware of his schemes to keep us bitter, resentful, offended, and unforgiving. This is "in order that Satan might not outwit us. For we are not unaware of his schemes" (2 Cor. 2:11). I thank God He is using the times when I have been outwitted for His good (Rom. 8:28).

I am coming full circle in learning to rest in the Lord's provision for the future of my publishing company and not trying to manage it myself.

For the first two years, I begrudgingly kept the plate of Redemption Press spinning. It got old to be spending a lot of time working and being the last one to take a paycheck, during a time when my new husband was wishing I would take more time off. I repeatedly asked God, *Can I please be done?*

There's a connection between not being obedient to what God asks us to do and deception. I looked for an "out" from the responsibilities of running the business, but it wasn't the Lord's timing, so I became vulnerable to being deceived. I considered turning the press over to a former acquaintance from Texas who led me to believe she had all the answers for taking Redemption Press to the next level. When I found out this wasn't true, she tried playing the "God card" to control me into continuing to pay her company $4,000 a month.

In looking back, I recognized when I was discontent and didn't want to do what God had called me to, I had become open to deception once again.

Once I embraced God's call and accepted the flock He has given me at Redemption Press as those I am to speak life into (not just all the people listening on the radio and reading my blog), the circumstances began to change. Clarity for the future and new business came in.

The still, small voice of the Holy Spirit had reminded me when I was neglecting those He'd given into my care as employees and team members. Once I embraced my assignment and repented for my neglect and lack of concern, circumstances made a turnaround in amazing ways.

So often in the past I would voice, "I want to change," or "I need to change," but didn't make the needed changes. This time, I had an overwhelming sense I was resenting the gift God had given me in Redemption Press. Convicted, I went to each staff member, one on one, and confessed, "I know I have hurt you," and then asked them specifically how I had done so.

I listened closely and saw things from a totally new perspective. I was grieved at how I'd hurt the very people who were loyal to me and worked hard for me.

My shift in attitude changed the way I treated my staff. I was no longer the person in charge who only paid them to do whatever I wanted and didn't care if they enjoyed it or not. I became a team player and allowed them to see my vulnerability. I let them know when I was scared about our finances instead of hiding it from them. I got off my high horse and started working alongside the team instead of hiding away in my "tower."

My godly sorrow and repentance spoke volumes. Some of my staff remarked, "You've really changed, Athena," telling me how much it inspired and encouraged them.

It wasn't until the spring of 2016 when I had a full shift in my attitude towards this call on my life and repented for resisting the commitment He had clearly called me to make. I embraced it with all the joy He provided. My work is now a place of ministry and refining and a blessing to me.

It is amazing to me how God has moved me from wanting to keep everyone at arm's length by just doing my ministry by writing and radio, while ignoring those under my care at Redemption Press and The Summit. He has brought me full circle to enjoying nurturing and developing relationships with the women under my care at work and at church. What an evidence of the faithfulness of God in my life! He has brought me from my old patterns of never fully trusting women to a place where I have learned to enjoy working alongside them.

I'm discovering I need to work *on* my business instead of just *in* it. I'm part of Dave Ramsey's Entreleadership coaching program and am learning not to be controlled by my day but to plan it instead. This is so *not* me—I am not a planner.

For instance, I'm scheduling specific times during the day to answer e-mail, while keeping my attention on the important things needing to be done. Instead of just reacting to whatever is screaming for attention, whatever is in front of me—the tyranny of the urgent—I am learning to be more purposeful. This relates to home tasks like cleaning, or grocery shopping, or women's ministry planning, and communicating for the next event, or getting my radio show ready, or working on the publishing proposals I need to create at Redemption, or prepping for the next NCWA meeting! It's so easy for me to react to whatever is the loudest but may not be what's profitable. I need to be more purposeful, which, by the way, is my word and overarching theme for 2017.

As I ponder and pray over what I need to accomplish for the day, I can then plan and put into practice what God has shown me. And to top it off, I can be fully present in doing so, not thinking of a million other things not getting done.

I want to make the most of every opportunity God gives me. Whether it's in business, ministry, home, marriage, or my family, I want to be purposeful in all I do. He created me on purpose, with a purpose.

And I have discovered—through everything I have experienced—when I surrender to His way, His purposes are always good.

In January 1995, I penned the following as a prayer, just a few years before my descent into deception.

The Desires of My Heart

To see my children on-fire for Jesus,
To be free from all unhealthy compulsive behavior,
To be used by God to touch hurting people for Him,
To be the mother and wife He created me to be,
To live a radical life of faith where God's presence and
provision are a daily occurrence.

While some of these prayers are still set before the Lord, I am learning to find my true home in Christ. To rest in His approval, His love.

Knowing how much God loves me, I am finding my significance in Him, rather than in what I do or with whom I am associated.

I have let go of all the false to find the true. In doing so, He has brought me true, lasting love, and returned my family to me.

The little girl who once cried out, "Look at me! See me!" is now saying, "Look what the Lord has done!"

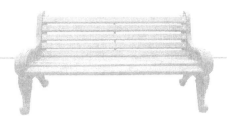

Recommended Reading

Spiritual Growth Resources

Balarie, Kelly. *Fear Fighting: Awakening Courage to Overcome Your Fears* (Baker Books, 2017).

Brown, Sharon Garlow. *Sensible Shoes: A Story About the Spiritual Journey* (InterVarsity Press, 2012).

Cowman, L. B. *Streams in the Desert*, James Reimann, ed. (Zondervan, 1997).

DeMuth, Mary. *Thin Places: A Memoir* (Zondervan, 2010).

Eno, Nick. *The Orphan Syndrome: Breaking Free and Finding Home* (Redemption Press, 2016).

Fleece, Esther. *No More Faking Fine: Ending the Pretending* (Zondervan, 2017).

Holleman, Heather. *Guarded by Christ: Knowing the God Who Rescues and Keeps Us* (Moody Publishers, 2016).

Johnson, Christy. *Love Junkies: 7 Steps to Breaking the Toxic Relationship Cycle* (Authentic Publishers, 2014).

Maples, Nika. *Hunting Hope: Dig Through the Darkness to Find the Light* (Worthy Inspired, 2016).

Niequist, Shauna. *Present over Perfect: Leaving Behind Frantic for a Simpler, More Soulful Way of Living* (Zondervan, 2016).

Pillar, Michele. *Untangled: The Truth Will Set You Free* (BroadStreet Publishing Group, 2016).

Ruchti, Cynthia. *Ragged Hope: Surviving the Fallout of Other People's Choices* (Abingdon Press, 2013).

Ruchti. *Tattered and Mended: The Art of Healing the Wounded Soul* (Abingdon Press, 2015).

Samples, Tina and Dena Dyer. *Wounded Women of the Bible: Finding Hope When Life Hurts* (Kregel Publications, 2013).

Story, Laura. *When God Doesn't Fix It: Lessons You Never Wanted to Learn—Truths You Can't Live Without* (W Publishing Group, 2015).

Voisey, Sheridan. *Resurrection Year: Turning Broken Dreams into New Beginnings* (Thomas Nelson, 2013).

Walsh, Sheila. *The Longing in Me: How Everything You Crave Leads to the Heart of God* (Nelson Books, 2016).

Woll, Mary Beth and Paul Meier. *Growing Stronger: 12 Guidelines Designed to Turn Your Darkest Hour into Your Greatest Victory* (Morgan James Publishing, 2015).

Resources for Healing from Spiritual Abuse

Anderson, Neil, Rich Miller, and Paul Travis. *Breaking the Bondage of Legalism* (Harvest House Publishers, 2003).

Arterburn, Stephen. *Faith that Hurts, Faith that Heals: Understanding the Fine Line Between Healthy Faith and Spiritual Abuse* (Thomas Nelson, 1993).

Arterburn, Stephen and Jack Felton. *Toxic Faith: Experiencing Healing from Painful Spiritual Abuse* (Shaw Books, 1991, 2001).

Chrnalogar, Mary Alice. *Twisted Scriptures: Breaking Free from Churches that Abuse* (Zondervan, 1997, 2000, rev. ed.).

Enroth, Ronald. *Churches that Abuse: Help for Those Hurt by Legalism: Authoritarian Leadership, and Spiritual Intimidation* (Zondervan, 1993). *Note:* Dr. Enroth has kindly given permission for full text editions of his two books on spiritual abuse to be available online at Apologetics Index: *Churches that Abuse* (1993) and its sequel, *Recovering from Churches that Abuse* (1994).

Enroth, Ronald. *Recovering from Churches that Abuse: The Road Back from Spiritual Abuse. Healing for Families who Hurt. Reentry for Survivors of Cults and Sects. Guidance for Pastors and Counselors* (Zondervan, 1994).

Johnson, David and Jeff VanVonderen. *The Subtle Power of Spiritual Abuse: Recognizing and Escaping Spiritual Manipulation and False Spiritual Authority Within the Church* (Bethany House, 1991, 2005).

Lawless, Agnes and John Lawless. *The Drift into Deception: The Eight Characteristics of Abusive Christianity* (Kregel Publications, 1995).

Webb, Mary Teresa. *Who's Calling? Ministry Discernment, Disasters, Restoration* (Redemption Press, 2015).

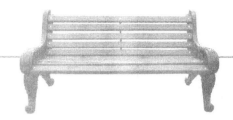

Acknowledgments

Let someone else praise you, and not your own mouth; an outsider, and not your own lips.

—Proverbs 27:2

To Inger Logelin. We go way back, almost thirty years. Without your help in bringing my blog posts, radio shows, and all the details of my story together, this book never would have happened. You've been a dear friend, valuable Redemption Press team member as senior editor, and gifted wordsmith in bringing my story to life. Thank you from the bottom of my heart.

To the Redemption Press team for supporting me as I proclaim the faithfulness of God through this book, my weekly radio show, and all my travels near and far. You have all been a huge blessing to me. Thank you specifically to Hannah MacKenzie who helped expedite the production of this book in time for the National Religious Broadcaster's 2017 convention.

To all those across the nation and around the world who have encouraged me to tell my story of God's faithfulness. Through social media, phone calls, e-mails and in person, so many of you have blessed me with prayers and confirmation. I am grateful.

And to my husband, Ross. You have supported me and affirmed me in the telling of my story and have been the hero of my modern-day Cinderella tale. I love you with everything in me.

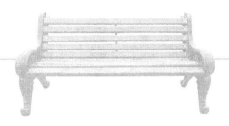

I'd love to hear from you about how God has brought
you full circle and been faithful in your life!

E-mail me at
athena@athenadeanholtz.com
or visit me at
athenadeanholtz.com.

If your church or women's ministry would like to have me
come and share my story of God's faithfulness,
contact me through Redemption Press at 360.226.3488

Order Information

To order additional copies of this book, please visit
www.redemption-press.com.
Also available on Amazon.com and BarnesandNoble.com
Or by calling toll free 1-844-2REDEEM.

Discounts available for bulk orders.